TOP SECRET

ALIEN ABDUCTION FILES

TOP SECRET
ALIEN
ABDUCTION
FILES

What the government doesn't want you to know

NICK REDFERN

disinformation®

Published by Disinformation Books, an imprint of
Red Wheel/Weiser, LLC
with offices at
65 Parker Street, Suite 7
Newburyport, MA 01950
www.redwheelweiser.com

ISBN: 978-1-938875-16-8
Library of Congress Cataloging-in-Publication Data

Names: Redfern, Nicholas, 1964- author.
Title: Top secret alien abduction files : what the government doesn't want
  you to know / Nick Redfern.
Description: Newburyport, MA : Disinformation Books, an imprint of Red Wheel/
  Weiser, LLC, [2018] | Includes bibliographical references.
Identifiers: LCCN 2018033908 | ISBN 9781938875168
Subjects: LCSH: Alien abduction--United States. | United States--Politics and government.
Classification: LCC BF2050 .R444 2018 | DDC 001.942--dc23
LC record available at https://lccn.loc.gov/2018033908

Cover design by Kathryn Sky-Peck
Interior photos/images by Nick Redfern
Interior by Gina Schenck
Typeset in Adobe Garamond Pro and Arial

Printed in Canada
MAR
10 9 8 7 6 5 4 3 2 1

CONTENTS

INTRODUCTION

We live in a world in which secret surveillance is becoming ever more dominating. Just about every bit of data on our smartphones can be secretly accessed. Our every online activity can be scrutinized behind closed doors. Even our smart TVs are wide open to hackers. And who is responsible? The government, of course. Regardless of what you or I think of the Edward Snowden affair and its attendant revelations, the fact is that Snowden demonstrated—to an extraordinary and disturbing degree—just how much of a *1984*-like society we have become. And in an incredibly short period of time, too. The National Security Agency (NSA) and other agencies of government have the ability to penetrate just about every aspect of our private lives: our medical records, where we take our vacations, what books we might buy on Amazon, and more are all issues that can be easily accessed with the right technology. But it's not just government that has taken us down a path to an Orwellian nightmare. The surveillance state is now a part of our culture, too: take, for example, the outrageous trend of companies now regularly demanding access to the passwords of the Facebook accounts of their employees.

Of course, the primary reason for such widespread spying—and lying about the spying—is due to the current state of the planet: the war on terror, in other words. When it comes to shutting down terrorist cells, finding and wiping out crazed bombers, and tracking down those who would do us harm, surveillance technology has achieved a great deal. The problem is, though, that it has gone too far. The lunatics are now running the asylum. Common sense has gone out the window. Does an eighty-year-old lady living with just her cat for company really need to be a victim of data collection? No. In other words, the surveillance has reached unwarranted, outrageous proportions.

All of which sets the scene for a study of another kind of surveillance, one which involves not terrorists of the foreign or domestic kind but none other than people who claim to have been taken away by extraterrestrials. We're talking about the alien abduction phenomenon. The government secretly spends vast amounts of money on monitoring those who claim to have been kidnapped by strange, unearthly beings with even stranger agendas.

Most people would laugh at such a scenario. They shouldn't, though: that is *exactly* what is going on. And it has been going on not just for years, but for decades. All around the world, people have reported close encounters with extraterrestrial entities. Witnesses describe being kidnapped in the dead of night by large-headed, black-eyed creatures from other worlds. Those same creatures have become popularly known as the Greys. People subjected to alien abduction typically report intrusive experiments that revolve around genetics, human reproduction, and even the creation of alien–human hybrids. There is, however, another aspect to the alien abduction controversy. And it is perhaps the most sinister aspect of all.

Abductees very often report being followed and spied upon by military and government personnel. It is typical for abductees to see black helicopters hovering directly over their homes. Mail is often intercepted. Letters are opened. Phone calls are monitored. Emails and social media are hacked. Strange men dressed in black suits photograph abductees' homes. All of which brings us to the matter of what has become known in the domain of alien abduction research as MILAB, or military abduction.

According to numerous accounts, after being kidnapped by alien entities, the abductees are shortly thereafter kidnapped *again . . . by the government.* These follow-up MILABS are the work of a powerful group hidden deep within the military and the intelligence community. It is the secret agenda of these highly classified organizations to figure out what the goal of the so-called Greys really is. And the best way for the government to get the answers is to interrogate and monitor those who have come face-to-face with the UFO phenomenon: the abductees, themselves. The questions this book asks—and answers—are important and paradigm changing:

1. Why is the government secretly compiling files on alien abductees?

2. Is the alien abduction issue so sinister that it has become a matter of national security?

3. How does the Department of Homeland Security (DHS) play a role in the secret surveillance of those who have had human–alien interaction?

4. Is the government concerned that the aliens are creating a sinister underground army of human–ET hybrids?

5. Who is flying the black helicopters?

6. Does the government know something we don't know?

7. What is the endgame?

In the pages of this book you will be confronted by case after case demonstrating how and why government agencies believe that the alien abduction phenomenon is indeed one which has to be watched carefully and constantly. Highlights include the following:

- One of the world's most famous alien abductions of all time, that of Betty and Barney Hill. They were abducted on the night of September 19, 1961, while returning to their New Hampshire home, after a vacation in Canada. Like so many abductees, the pair was subjected to stressful, intrusive medical procedures onboard a UFO. Their abductors were nonhuman things with penetrating, staring eyes. The US Air Force soon opened a file on the Hill affair that details their extraordinary experience.

- The May 23, 1973, alien abduction of Judy Doraty, who encountered a disk-shaped UFO while driving near Houston, Texas, late at night. After having a series of bad dreams, it became clear to Doraty that there was a period of "missing time" in her recollections of what had happened to her. Upon being hypnotized by UFO researcher Dr. Leo Sprinkle, Doraty recalled the portion of the event which had been almost completely erased from her mind. She described seeing a calf being taken aboard the UFO, "like it's being sucked up." Doraty also recalled being taken onboard the craft. In no time at all, the Air Force Office of Special Investigations (AFOSI) at Kirtland Air Force Base in New Mexico opened a secret file on Doraty and her experience—something which was prompted by the unique nature of her kidnapping. Namely, that Doraty was abducted because she had stumbled upon a so-called "cattle mutilation" event. The implication being that the ETs tried to wipe her memory clean, as a means to prevent her from revealing what she had encountered. The AFOSI was deeply concerned by the cattle mutilation/alien abduction connection, as will become apparent.

- Charles Hickson and Calvin Parker's late-night kidnapping from the banks of the Pascagoula River in October 1973. They recalled, under hypnosis, being taken onboard a UFO by creatures with "lobster-like claws." The pair became the subject of intense scrutiny by military personnel at Keesler Air Force Base in Mississippi. Intelligence staff at Keesler kept a careful watch on Hickson and Parker for months, secretly monitoring their activities.

- Myrna Hansen's encounter of May 5, 1980, which occurred as she was heading to Eagle's Nest, New Mexico, after a road trip to Oklahoma. Hansen experienced a classic alien abduction experience. Notably, and just like Judy Doraty seven years earlier, Hansen saw a young cow being "sucked" into a UFO. More intriguing, Hansen recalled being taken to an underground facility, where aliens implanted her with a sophisticated tracking device. When Hansen described the appearance of the facility, it quickly caught the attention of the AFOSI at Kirtland Air Force Base. There was a very good reason for this: the facility she described was an off-limits underground bunker at the base's weapons storage area; the implication being that the military and the ETs may have been secretly working together, deep underground. Extensive files were opened on Hansen's experience.

- The government's targeting of UFO researcher Greg Bishop and the late alien abductee Dr. Karla Turner. In the mid-1990s, Bishop struck up a friendship with Turner, who was the author of a number of books on her experiences, including *Into the Fringe*. As this was, largely, the pre-internet era, the pair corresponded by mail. As Bishop revealed after Turner's death, mail sent to and from the pair arrived already opened—torn and resealed. On other occasions, the letters weren't even resealed. Both Bishop and Turner were convinced this was all part of some mind manipulation program, a government-driven operation designed to psychologically destabilize the pair by letting them know that the government was watching them.

- Accounts from numerous abductees reporting encounters with "black helicopters." For years, abductees have reported close encounters with not just UFOs and aliens, but with what have become infamously known as "black helicopters." These usually unmarked crafts are reported flying over the homes of abductees.

On occasion, they will hover over the same homes for minutes at a time, and at precariously low levels. Typically, they turn up within a day or two of an alien abduction experience. All of the evidence suggests that the helicopters are piloted by "black ops" teams who have three primary goals: (1) to determine the range and scope of alien abductions; (2) to frighten the abductees into staying quiet about their experiences; and (3) to figure out the extraterrestrial agenda. The black helicopter–based experiences of numerous people are addressed, including those of abductee Betty Andreasson, one of the most famous figures in ufology, as well as the journalist Ed Conroy, who became a victim of black helicopter invasions after publishing a book about Whitley Strieber's alien abduction.

- A study of the claims that deep within the heart of the Department of Homeland Security (DHS) there exists a small group that secretly, and actively, monitors the alien abduction issue. Much of this is undertaken by keeping a careful watch on social media (primarily Facebook and Twitter), as well as websites, blogs, lectures, conferences, and books. DHS is secretly compiling an extensive database of alien abductees in the United States. On occasion, DHS agents have visited the homes of abductees, warning them not to talk about their UFO abduction experiences. In recent years, such actions may have been interpreted as so-called Men in Black encounters.

- A careful examination of the MILAB, or military abduction, phenomenon, which has been escalating in the twenty-first century. Many abductees report that after being kidnapped by ETs, they are soon abducted by other forces. Not aliens, but military personnel who are usually dressed in black SWAT-style outfits. Those who have reported such experiences describe being taken to underground installations, where they are interrogated and questioned about their encounters. Military personnel reveal to the abductees the government's belief that the aliens are creating "underground armies" of abductees who, when fully mind-controlled by the aliens, will one day turn upon the rest of the population. In other words, at the heart of the MILAB phenomenon is a worrying belief that the alien agenda is based around massive mind manipulation and control.

Come with me now, as we peel away the layers of a conspiracy that has existed since the 1950s and which, today, and as a result of large-scale surveillance techniques and technology, is bigger than ever. And it shows no sign of stopping.

1 BEFORE THE ABDUCTEES THERE WERE THE CONTACTEES

The idea that agencies of the US government, the military, and the intelligence community are actively and secretly monitoring Americans who have been subjected to the alien abduction experience may sound outlandish to many—perhaps even paranoid. The startling reality, however, is that such a situation is not at all outlandish. Nor is it paranoia driven. In fact, quite the opposite is the case. It's very important to note that there is an amazing precedent to the alien abduction controversy and its connections to government spying. It all revolves around what is known as the contactee phenomenon, which has its origins in the early 1950s.

It was in the summer of 1947—specifically June 24—when the UFO phenomenon began. That was the date on which the first report of an encounter with a flying saucer occurred. The witness was a pilot named Kenneth Arnold. He encountered a squadron of such craft near Mt. Rainier, Washington state. In the days and months that followed, more and more sightings of such craft occurred: a phenomenon was born that is still very much with us to this day. But in those early days, the UFOs hardly ever landed. Even when they did, their crews never exited their craft. That all changed in the early 1950s when—after a few years of deliberately staying behind a curtain of secrecy—they slowly but surely showed themselves.

The Differences Between Contactees and Abductees

Long before the first alien abduction incident was reported, elements of the US government were *already* secretly monitoring certain figures in the United States who claimed close encounters with extraterrestrials. Agencies were carefully collating files, listening in on phone calls, and intercepting the mail of dozens of people. Those same figures became known as the contactees. It's important to have an understanding of the contactee phenomenon, as it serves to demonstrate how and why it led government, military, and intelligence personnel to focus on the claims of ET interaction—and then to do precisely the same when the abduction issue took off.

Most of the secret work in the contactee field was carried out in the 1950s. It was undertaken to learn what was allegedly being done to American citizens by our mysterious visitors. At the time, the bulk of the work fell under the auspices of the Federal Bureau of Investigation (FBI), and at the express order of none other than almost-legendary FBI director J. Edgar Hoover. How do we know this? Simple: thanks to legislation brought about under the Freedom of Information Act, numerous files on the contactees have now been released into the public domain. Real *X-Files*? You bet. Those files make it abundantly clear that the US government went to extraordinary steps to ensure that the contactees were placed under careful, secret watch—particularly because those contactees were clearly influencing public opinion on matters relative to not just alien visitations but also politics, the economy, and religion.

Before we get to the matter of demonstrating how and why the contactees became such a potential threat to the government, it's important to first demonstrate the differences between the contactees and the abductees. The abduction experience is almost always a traumatic one: people are kidnapped and taken away against their will. They are subjected to horrific and trauma-filled experiments that revolve around matters related to human reproduction, DNA, sex, and even alien–human hybridization. The Greys of modern-day ufology are described as emotionless, cold creatures. They may actually be highly sophisticated, biological robots designed and programmed to perform endless numbers of abductions, and all to fulfill their still not fully understood agenda. Their appearances—wizened, dwarfish things with oily-black eyes—provoke terror in many who have had the misfortune to cross their paths.

Compared to all of that, the contactees got off lightly. *Extremely* lightly. All of the above is in stark contrast to the goals and the actions of the extraterrestrial beings encountered by the contactees. The Space Brothers— which is the title given to the particular group of aliens that the contactees claimed interaction with—were physically almost identical to us, the human race. That is, aside from a few very minor differences in their physical appearance. As for the agenda of the Space Brothers, it was very different from that of the Greys: hideous experiments were nowhere in sight. No one was ever taken aboard a UFO against their will. And minds were not wiped clean of memories of the alien kind. All that the Space Brothers wanted was for humanity to unite as one, to live without war, and to pledge allegiance to the world, rather than to any specific nation, culture, or belief system. Too good to be true? Maybe. On the other hand, though, maybe not. Let's take a look at the stories of the contactees, their liaisons with the Space Brothers, and the top secret response of the US government and its ever-growing number of secret files on those who claimed contact with aliens.

The Phenomenon Takes Off with a Man Named Adamski

There is no doubt at all that the most well known, visible, and controversial of all the early contactees was George Adamski. Born just a few years before the dawning of the twentieth century, Adamski was a Polish man who immigrated to the United States with his family when he was barely out of the cradle. At an early age, Adamski gravitated to an alternative lifestyle: after a period serving in the US military, Adamski worked a variety of jobs, none of which brought him the satisfaction, or publicity, he sorely craved. That all changed, however, when in the 1930s he headed out to the city of Laguna Beach, California.

It was in Laguna Beach that Adamski created what he termed the Royal Order of Tibet. The *Los Angeles Times* referred to Adamski's retreat as "Shamanistic" in nature. In turn, Adamski assured readers that "I do not bring to Laguna the weird rites and bestial superstition in which the old Lamaism is steeped, but the scientific portions of the religion." For around six years, the Royal Order of Tibet thrived—after which Adamski and his followers moved to Palomar Mountain, in northern San Diego County. Palomar Gardens was quickly created to ensure a peaceful, relaxing vibe for those who wished to opt out from the rat race—and there were plenty of them. Then, in October 1946, Adamski and several of his followers said they encountered a huge alien spacecraft flying high in the skies over the mountain, which was close to a year *before* the first acknowledged flying saucer encounter was reported by Kenneth Arnold. It was, however, in late 1952 that Adamski's involvement in the UFO scene really took off.

A Meeting of Minds—One of Them Nonhuman

In the early hours of November 20, 1952, Adamski and his secretary, Lucy McGinnis, headed out of Palomar Mountain and drove to Blythe, California. It was all as a result of a sudden, out-of-the-blue hunch that Adamski had—one which led him to believe that a close encounter was looming on the horizon. As dawn broke, they met with several fellow saucer seekers: Al and Betty Bailey, and George Hunt Williamson, who was a fellow contactee who also caught the secret attention of the FBI, as we shall soon see.

After breakfast, Adamski had an eerie feeling that the group needed to head off to Parker, Arizona, which they quickly did. It wasn't long before one and all were shocked and amazed by the sight of a huge, silver-colored

UFO that was "cigar"-like in shape and maneuvering high in the clear skies over Parker. An excited Adamski shouted to the group to follow it, and they raced for their cars and hit the dirt road in pursuit of the craft from another world. According to Adamski and his friends, the craft shot out of the area after being pursued by a squadron of military aircraft. Soon after, though, a much smaller flying saucer–type vehicle landed on a nearby mountain. For Adamski, this was a sign the aliens wanted to converse with him, face-to-face. That, we're told, is exactly what happened. As the rest of the group kept their distance, Adamski tentatively walked toward the alien craft. A door on the vehicle opened, and Adamski, holding his breath, was confronted by a long-haired human-looking figure dressed in a one-piece suit, not unlike the kind of outfit worn by today's military pilots.

Adamski said the long-haired human-looking being claimed his name was Orthon, that he came from the planet Venus, and that he was here to warn the world of the perils of nuclear weapons. Orthon told the excited and shocked Adamski that he, Adamski, was to be a part of a worldwide program designed to push human civilization away from planetwide annihilation and toward a new paradise. With that all said, Orthon returned to his flying saucer, which raced into the heavens and vanished from view.

In mere minutes, Adamski was a new man with a new plan. He claimed further controversial encounters with the Space Brothers and, in 1953, coauthored with Desmond Leslie a book on the entire affair titled *Flying Saucers Have Landed*. The book proved to be a huge hit, selling more than 100,000 copies in no time at all. Adamski had gone from a figure of relative obscurity to one that countless numbers of people were listening to—and listening to very carefully. Those listeners included none other than some of the finest special agents of the FBI.

One of the Strangest FBI Dossiers of All

It's important to note that the stories of George Adamski—who died in 1965—have both believers and disbelievers. That Orthon looked extremely human and claimed to be a Venusian has had many a UFO researcher rolling their eyes—and quite understandably. On the other hand, Adamski still has a faithful following to this day which shows no signs of going away anytime soon. For the FBI, though, it wasn't so much whether Adamski's claims were true or not. Rather, it was the influence that Adamski was having on the American public that had them worried. Deeply so, too.

Had Adamski just told his readers, and listeners, tales of exciting encounters with spacemen and spacewomen from other worlds, then, in all probability, the FBI would not have cared. But things *didn't* end there. According to Adamski, his aliens were communists. He claimed that the Soviet way of life was also the way of the future. That the Russians would be the victors in a looming Third World War, and that the Space Brothers would then usher in a new era in which alien communists would sculpt a new Earth.

Today, much of this might sound farcical and far-fetched, but the thousands upon thousands of people who completely bought into all this had the FBI concerned. As a result, J. Edgar Hoover ordered a file to be opened on Adamski. It ran from 1952 to 1965, amounts to around 130 pages, and is now available under Freedom of Information legislation. The file makes it very clear that the Bureau was far from impressed by anything Adamski had to say about his alleged alien encounters. The issue of how Adamski insisted on spreading the word of communism, though— and doing so via the message and the medium of the Space Brothers— continued to worry and vex the FBI. The bureau even speculated on the possibility that the Russians had staged the UFO encounter in Parker, Arizona—possibly to the point of using a Soviet agent posing as an alien! Even more troubling to the FBI was the fact that in the wake of Adamski's claims, more and more people reported very similar encounters. One of them was George Van Tassel. He, too, would soon become the subject of a government file.

The FBI and Ancient Extraterrestrials

Born in 1910, George Van Tassel had a deep interest in aviation as a child and teenager—and he eventually paved for himself a good career at Hughes

TO: DIRECTOR, FBI   5-28-52
     SD 100- 8325

so much more advanced than the inhabitants of this earth that
they have deciphered the languages used here. ADAMSKI stated
that in this interplanetary communication, the Federal Communications Commission asked the inhabitants of the other planet concerning the type of government they had there and the reply indicated that it was very different from the democracy of the
United States. ADAMSKI stated that his answer was kept secret
by the United States Government, but he added, "If you ask me
they probably have a Communist form of government and our
American government wouldn't release that kind of thing, naturally.
That is a thing of the future - more advanced."

ADAMSKI advised ▆▆▆▆ that he wants to set up his
own radio station in order to communicate with the inhabitants
of other planets, but that to do so would cost him approximately
$5,000. Commenting on observation and study at Palomar Observa-
torn, ADAMSKI stated "Everything is bottlenecked" at the Observa-
torn, and "they won't let anybody know of their findings with
their lar   scope because it would make all the textbooks
obsolete".

ADAMSKI, during this conversation, made the prediction
that Russia will dominate the world and we will then have an era
of peace for 1000 years. He stated that Russia already has the
atom bomb and the hydrogen bomb and that the great earthquake
which was reported behind the Iron Curtain recently was actually
a hydrogen bomb explosion being tried out by the Russians.
ADAMSKI states this "earthquake" broke seismograph machines and
he added that no normal earthquake can do that.

ADAMSKI stated that within the next twelve months,
San Diego will be bombed. ADAMSKI stated that it does not make
any difference if the United States has more atom bombs than
Russia inasmuch as Russia needs only ten atom bombs to cripple
the United States by placing these simultaneously on such spots
as Chicago and other vital centers of this country.

ADAMSKI further stated that the United States today
is in the same state of deterioration as was the Roman empire
prior to its collapse and it will fall just as the Roman empire
did. He stated the Government in this country is a corrupt form
of government and capitalists are enslaving the labor.

- 2 -

A page from the FBI's file on contactee George Adamski (courtesy of the Federal Bureau of Investigation)

Aircraft, where he came to be good friends with none other than aviation legend, and certifiable loon, Howard Hughes. Just like Adamski, Van Tassel felt compelled to make a move to California. In his case, it was to the small town of Landers, which is situated in the Mojave Desert. On one particular night in August 1953, so Van Tassel claimed, he was overwhelmed by a sense that he had to drive out to a nearby area known as Giant Rock. The locale takes its name from a huge mass of rock, which still stands in the area to this day, albeit now somewhat battered and bruised.

Van Tassel knew that something important was going to happen, but exactly what, he wasn't too sure. He soon found out, though. Just like the other George, Van Tassel was confronted by a flying saucer that descended from the heavens and delivered several aliens looking just like us. As with Adamski's initial encounter, Van Tassel was also fed information suggesting that the ETs were communists and wanted our world radically transformed. There are a few indications from what Van Tassel said and wrote that the aliens were somewhat bully-like in nature, too, specifically when it got down to the issue of wanting things to go their way. Then, as mysteriously as they appeared, the aliens were gone, vanished into the dark skies above Giant Rock and the sprawling desert landscape.

Practically overnight, Van Tassel's life changed dramatically. Whereas Adamski chose to write books about his experiences, Van Tassel decided to hold annual UFO conferences out at Giant Rock, which continued until his death in 1977. At the height of their popularity, the Giant Rock gigs had audiences in excess of *ten thousand*. No wonder the FBI thought Van Tassel, like Adamski, should be watched—and watched closely, too. The aliens, Van Tassel said, had another task for him: they ordered him to build what became known as the Integratron—a large, white, circular, two-level building that would have the ability to slow the aging process—in Landers, California. At least, that's how he told it. Unfortunately, Van Tassel passed away before the Integratron was fully completed.

The FBI's surveillance file on Van Tassel exceeds 300 pages and demonstrates that FBI agents visited Van Tassel on three occasions in the 1950s. While the meetings were quite cordial, the FBI was troubled by

George Van Tassel's Integratron (Nick Redfern)

how Van Tassel was suggesting in his phenomenally well-attended lectures that certain events described in the pages of the Bible—such as the parting of the Red Sea, the story of Noah and the Ark, and the fall of the walls of Jericho—were all connected to ancient visitations from extraterrestrials and not the work of God. Those same agents noted in their reports to Hoover that the aliens wished to reinvent the US economy. For the bureau, this all very much paralleled what George Adamski was also saying. No wonder, then, that Van Tassel became what, today, is ominously known as "a person of interest."

A Catalog of Contactees

Other contactees who were also watched by the FBI—and specifically because of the political overtones attached to their accounts of alien visitation and interaction—included Truman Bethurum, who, in 1952, maintained he had close encounters with a beautiful alien woman known as Aura Rhanes; Orfeo Angelucci, a man who also spread the word that communism was not a bad thing, after all; George Hunt Williamson, who was a friend of Adamski; and Frank Stranges, who claimed that benign extraterrestrials had infiltrated the heart of the Pentagon and the US government.

It was much the same overseas, too. For example, in the late 1950s, an arm of the British police force called Special Branch—which today largely handles cases of domestic terrorism—began secretly watching the Aetherius Society. It was a contactee-driven group created in 1954 by an Englishman named George King. He too claimed encounters with aliens who, physically, could pass for us.

The United Kingdom's Freedom of Information Act has shown that George King and his Aetherius Society were the subject of a secret Special Branch file which ran to dozens of pages. And as Special Branch saw it, there was a damn good reason for that: according to King, his alien buddies had informed him that we all needed to disarm our nuclear arsenals. If we didn't, there would be nothing but death and disaster for one and all. When members of the Aetherius Society took to the streets of London in 1958 and 1959 to make their views on nuclear weapons known, Special Branch agents were in the crowds, listening to and noting every word.

Why the Contactees Are Important to the Abduction Issue

What all of this demonstrates is that secret government interest in the claims of people who say they have met aliens dates back more than sixty years, that agencies of government quietly opened files on those same people, and that the surveillance was due to the concerns the FBI and the Special Branch had about the contactees suggesting that our visitors from the stars were commies.

Whatever any of us might think about the controversial claims of the contactees of the 1950s, there's no denying the *extremely* important fact

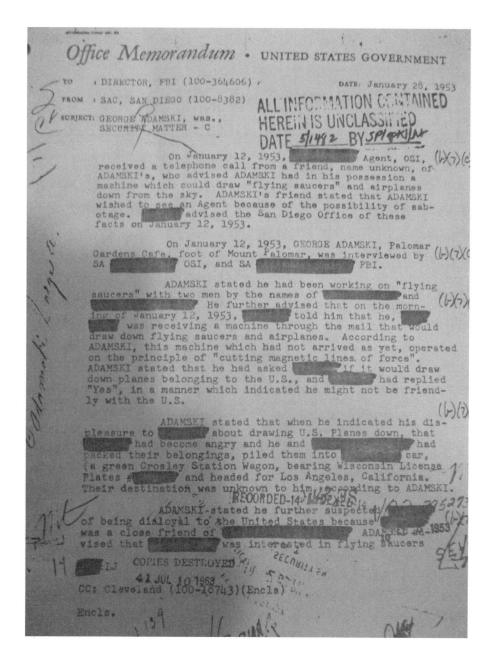

A 1953 FBI document on the September 1961 abduction of Betty and Barney Hill (courtesy of the US Air Force)

that it was those same claims which prompted government agencies to boost their investigations into, and surveillance of, those who specifically came *after* the contactees. I am, of course, talking about alien abductees and their accounts of the Greys. The hippie-like, peace-loving, flowing-haired extraterrestrials of the 1950s were about to be elbowed out of the picture by just about the most sinister, otherworldly creatures imaginable. And the files just grew and grew—as we'll see.

It's time to address one of the weirdest and mysterious UFO incidents of all, which involved an alien abduction not from someone's bedroom or car—as is so often reported—but from the skies above.

2 THE MEN WHO GOT CARRIED AWAY

The vast majority of all alien abduction cases have one thing in common: the abductee is returned to their home or vehicle after the experience. In a few cases, however, the person is never seen again. They're gone. As in forever. A perfect example is the weird and complicated saga of two men whose UFO research ended with them vanishing off the face of the planet. They were Karl Hunrath and Wilbur Wilkinson, relatively minor cogs in the UFO research wheel of the early 1950s, but men whose story is highly relevant to the world of extraterrestrial abductions today. To government files, also.

Both Hunrath and Wilkinson lived in Racine, Wisconsin. Hunrath was a loner, someone who was known for his hair-trigger character and his unfathomable loathing of women. Wilkinson, meanwhile, was very different: he was a laidback character and had a wife and kids; they absolutely defined what it was to be a family in 1950s America. Wilkinson and Hunrath, then, were poles apart in terms of their lives and their characters, but they had one thing that bonded them: a fascination for the growing flying saucer phenomenon. Hunrath, at the time, worked for a Racine-based company called the John Oster Manufacturing Company, which made kitchen appliances. It paid the bills, but that was nowhere near enough for Hunrath. He wanted out, he wanted excitement, and he wanted to be the man who solved the UFO riddle. Wilkinson was as interested in the saucer phenomenon as Hunrath, but he lacked his friend's get-up-and-go.

While Wilkinson just wanted answers as to what the aliens were, where they were from, and what they wanted, Hunrath wanted to uncover the truths surrounding their technology: What was it that powered flying saucers? How could those same craft perform left- and right-hand turns at hundreds—maybe even *thousands*—of miles per hour? Did they possess destructive weapons far beyond our atomic arsenals? If he was to stand even a small chance of getting the answers, Hunrath knew he had to make a move to UFO Central: California. So Hunrath—a ticking time bomb at the best of times—gave his boss the finger, emptied his bank account, and hit the road to Los Angeles. And he told Wilbur that if he really wanted to find the truth of alien visitations, then he'd better move to California, too. For a while, Wilkinson dithered, but eventually, and just like a dutiful puppy, he followed his master across the country. Fortunately for Wilkinson, his family was quite enthused about a move to the West Coast. In no time, one and all were settled in Los Angeles apartments. The lives of Hunrath and Wilkinson were about to change in the strangest way possible.

The first thing that happened was that the two men hooked up with just about all of the ufological players in California, which included George Adamski and George Van Tassel—two men who, as we have seen, had secret files opened on them by the FBI. They also became friendly with another of the contactees: George Hunt Williamson of Arizona, who was also a subject of scrutiny by J. Edgar Hoover's finest. It's hardly surprising, then, that the FBI soon opened records on Hunrath and Wilkinson as well. But let's not get too far ahead of ourselves: let's see how things started out.

A Stranger Pays a Visit

The FBI's papers on Wilkinson amount to just a few biographical notes and background checks—that's about it. The Hunrath file, however, is a very different kettle of fish. It's packed with odd nuggets of material—all of it saucer-themed. The papers reveal something very weird: in January 1952, just before the two men headed off to California, Hunrath had a strange close encounter in his bedroom in the twilight hours. There was not a bug-eyed alien in sight, though. What was there, rather, was a very human-looking being who appeared to have broken into Hunrath's home and, as he slept, injected him with an armful of chemicals. Not surprisingly, he was very quickly wide awake. God knows what those chemicals were, but they had a major effect on Hunrath.

Hunrath may have been wide awake, but there was something wrong—something very wrong: he felt spaced out and his head spun. And he couldn't move. All he could see was a tall, thin man dressed in a dark suit looming over the bed. In a fashion that echoed the experiences of Adamski and Van Tassel, Hunrath's intruder said something along the lines of "I am Bosco. You have been chosen to enter our brotherhood of galaxies." Hunrath noted that the alien had a curious accent; it was not unlike that of a European.

Just like every contactee under the sun, Hunrath was warned that our warlike ways would very soon get us into a catastrophic confrontation with the Soviets. Atomic annihilation, in other words, was just about on the doorsteps of everyone. The suit-and-tie-wearing Mr. Bosco—who came across like actor Michael Rennie's character Klaatu in the movie *The Day the Earth Stood Still*—told Hunrath that he, along with many others, had been chosen to help the aliens prevent the end of the world from coming—and from coming very soon. That is, if nothing was done about it. Supposedly, the aliens had "noticed" Hunrath's interest in UFOs—although how they knew that was anyone's guess.

According to what was referred to in the FBI files as "occult techniques," Hunrath's mind was filled with data on UFOs, their technologies, and their mission on our planet. And for what was said to be a benign, peaceful race, Bosco chose to share with Hunrath information on how to destroy Russian aircraft! But that was not enough for Bosco: he told Hunrath that the technology could also be used to bring down American military planes, too. For Bosco, Hunrath was to be his vessel, so to speak. Supposedly, Hunrath's mind was immediately flooded with all manner of technical and science-based imagery designed to help him create his very own weapons of mass destruction. With that, Bosco retreated to the shadows of the bedroom, opened the window, climbed out, and vanished into the night!

Hunrath was now a man on a mission—hence the quick decision to move to California. It was this encounter in the bedroom which convinced Hunrath to pack his belongings and get on the road. Quickly.

Controversy dogged Hunrath and Wilkinson big-time in their new city. They were visited on several occasions by agents of the FBI—the police, too. The neighbors complained of late-night banging in Hunrath's apartment—as if someone was constructing something in the dead of night. Perhaps it was that aircraft-destroying device that Hunrath was under the orders of Mr. Bosco to create. Hunrath was not at all intimidated, though. He denied that anything strange was going on. And he promised to keep the noise down—a promise he all but instantly broke.

When Wilkinson got a visit, however, he freaked out. All he wanted to do was find the truth about UFOs, and now the Feds were on his tail. Hunrath told him to develop a backbone. It didn't work.

Telepathic Powers and a Man from Space

Now it's time to take a look at the connections between Hunrath and Wilkinson and the aforementioned George Hunt Williamson—who was already "known" to the FBI because of rumors that he was smuggling ancient priceless artifacts across the US–Mexico border into the United States and then selling them for a tidy price.

Williamson was a curious character. He used several different names, including Michael d'Obrenovic and Brother Philip. Born in Chicago in 1926, he became entranced by the world of the unexplained before he was even a teenager. And when flying saucers exploded on the scene in the summer of 1947, it was all but inevitable that Williamson would dive into the controversy headfirst without looking back.

16

Williamson met with Hunrath and Wilkinson on a couple of occasions, at his Arizona home. It has to be said, though, that Williamson never considered the pair close friends. For Williamson, Wilkinson came across as meek and annoying, while Hunrath intimidated and even frightened Williamson with his abrasive style and character. But we do have a few important pieces of data on the pair from Williamson, particularly in relation to Hunrath. In a 1954 letter to a friend in ufology, Frank Gibson, Williamson writes:

Before Hunrath arrived in California he had become acquainted with another so-called "genius"—from Ohio. [Author's note: the first "genius" was Mr. Bosco.] This man called Karl one night saying he had just returned from Japan where he had been working with a Dr. Nagata on electromagnetic experiments. He asked Karl if he could come up to see him since he had heard that Karl was interested in magnetic research. The man came and he stayed four days and nights! When he left, Karl had become an avid saucer enthusiast. Karl said he thought the man was a "spaceman" because he answered his questions before they were asked and displayed telepathic powers.

So, what we have here is Hunrath having meetings with not one but two humanlike extraterrestrials, and both in relation to alien technology.

Hunrath Looks for Answers

Two enigmatic characters, both alleged aliens: one named Bosco, who was intent on destroying the US military, and the other a mysterious doctor jetting off to Japan to discuss matters relative to electromagnetic mysteries with that nation's scientists. And both of them had one person in their sights: Karl Hunrath. But what did Visitor Number Two have to do with Ohio? Hunrath wanted to know. Quickly. First, there is the location.

Dayton, Ohio—home to this mysterious "genius" according to George Hunt Williamson—was, and still is, *also* home to Wright-Patterson Air

Force Base. For years, it operated as the US government's very own UFO Central. Yep: Area 51, Nevada, hasn't always owned the copyright on that puppy. The Roswell bodies, recovered alien technology, secret files on alien autopsies—the rumor mill is that they were all stored at Wright-Pat for decades before finally being shipped out to the Nevada desert. Or maybe deep below it, behind the closed doors of a fortified bunker (or several).

Now, it's time to return to what George Hunt Williamson knew about all this. As a result of having made contact with one allegedly learned soul from Ohio (or from the stars), and having read rumors of crashed UFOs stashed away at Wright-Patterson—chiefly those rumors contained in Frank Scully's mighty but dubious tome of 1950, *Behind the Flying Saucers*—Hunrath, on his Kerouac-style trek to California, made a winding detour to Ohio and began asking all sorts of probing questions about flying saucers among Dayton's scientific community. There *was* a method to Hunrath's actions, even if it wasn't overly obvious to some of those he grilled.

The man of the hour was no fool. Hunrath, looking for an inroad to what officialdom *really* knew about UFOs, was well aware that if he shouted loud enough—in the one place on the map where the US government's innermost secrets of the UFO kind were said to be held, and where his alleged alien doctor/buddy was hanging out—someone would surely sit up and take notice sometime soon. And particularly so when he spread rumors around Dayton that, as a result of his growing research into alien technology, he had successfully created his wacky, airplane-obliterating contraption—which, very oddly, Hunrath was now calling "Bosco," after that mysterious intruder in the night. And Hunrath insisted on writing it in capitals: "BOSCO."

Yes, Hunrath *was* now spelling it with capitals, and he *was* talking about it as if it were some sort of machine-based, intelligent entity in its own right. But it was not alien aircraft—Hunrath told anyone and everyone in Dayton who would listen—that BOSCO was going to destroy. Not even Russian aircraft. *It was Uncle Sam's aircraft.* And, said Hunrath, in an almost proud fashion, he could not care less if the US military's planes fell like flies as a result of his actions. It was all, he believed, for the greater good and for the long-term survival of the human race. Why? Because the Space Brothers said so, that's why. Screw the FBI and their intimidating visit, Hunrath concluded. He was long gone, and Hoover's mob would never know he was shouting his mouth off in Ohio. Wrong.

Words from Williamson

Of course someone sat up and took notice when Hunrath started on about his plans to knock US Air Force planes out the air for the apparently less-than-friendly Space Brothers. Actually, when Hunrath got on his rant, quite a few people straightened their backs, opened their ears, and put on their government-regulation suits, fedora hats, and black sunglasses. Hunrath did not know it right away, but even before he reached the West Coast he was being closely watched by men dressed in black. (What other color could it really be?)

In early to-mid-1952, Hunrath finally reached Los Angeles and wasted no time at all in hooking up with the major UFO players in and around town, as George Hunt Williamson recalled to Frank Gibson: "It was in the winter of 1952 that I first met Karl at George Adamski's on Mount Palomar. . . . During the next few months he visited many saucer researchers including: Frank Scully, Gene Dorsey, George Van Tassel . . . and he was my house guest in Prescott, Arizona for a week."

Williamson continued:

He [Hunrath] was a strange man who would change his mind and ideas from one moment to the next. You couldn't help but like him, but at times a feeling would come over you that made you wish there were a million miles between yourself and Mr. Hunrath. Everyone who came in contact with him had the same experience. He visited saucer researchers as a friend, then, systematically began to spread rumors about them and their work, which had no basis in fact. He came to California unknown and soon was stirring up dissension wherever he went. Was it his purpose to cause trouble in the "hot-bed" of controversy

*existing among the California saucer enthusiasts? Was it part of a plan
formulated by negative forces? Why was Hunrath a brilliant scientist
one moment and a not too bright electrician the next?*

Hunrath Causes Trouble for Adamski

Williamson wasn't the only one looking for answers about Hunrath's intentions. The G-men of the Los Angeles office of the FBI were soon knocking on doors, too, and wanting to know what the hell Hunrath's game was. It turned out that on one fateful day in the summer of 1952 George Adamski's secretary, Lucy McGinnis, called the soon-to-be wife of one Jerrold Baker—a handyman at Palomar and one of Adamski's faithful friends—in alarmed fashion. Adamski, Hunrath, Wilkinson, and Baker had all been hanging out at Palomar that morning, harmlessly spending time trying to outdo each other in the UFO stakes. All was fine for a while, but matters nearly came to blows when Hunrath started ranting and bragging about how he—or more correctly, BOSCO—could destroy the US Air Force's aerial armada in a flash. Demonstrating a high degree of astuteness, Adamski became instantly concerned that this information might get back to law enforcement officials; he slung Hunrath, Wilkinson, and Baker off his property, ordering them never to return. It wasn't long before Adamski's worst nightmare came absolutely true.

Jerrold Baker's beloved, Irma, was unsure what to do about Lucy McGinnis's revelations concerning Hunrath and his boasting about being able to destroy American planes. So she erred on the side of what she perceived to be caution. That's to say, she picked up the phone, called the Air Force and the FBI, and spilled the beans. The whole damned can. Officialdom moved quickly and right in the direction of George Adamski. On arriving at his home later that very same day, the grim, unsmiling minions of J. Edgar Hoover told a quaking, fear-filled Adamski they had heard rumors that he, Adamski, "had in his possession a machine which could draw 'flying saucers' and airplanes down from the sky," which is a direct quote from the Hoover files on Hunrath. Rather oddly, the FBI clearly got its wires crossed when its agents said they had heard that the BOSCO machine was to arrive in the mail!

Although this latter point was completely untrue, Adamski realized immediately that the FBI agents were actually talking about Hunrath. Adamski corrected the agents and said that no, BOSCO was *not* coming via the Post Office—it was in Hunraths's hands already. Quite reasonably, the question might be asked, why not bring Hunrath in for questioning and settle matters, once and for all, regarding the man and his curiously named machine-friend, BOSCO? Simple: there were rumors floating around the FBI—which even George Hunt Williamson mysteriously managed to get a hold of, though how is a mystery unlikely to ever be resolved—that Hunrath had been secretly recruited by the Soviets to seek out the truth about flying saucers under the guise of simply being interested in the subject. But, if that *was* the case, then it was apparent to the bureau that Hunrath had to be a very small fish in a pond populated, somewhere in its murky depths, by extremely large fish of a red color that were secretly pulling the strings. So, the plan was to sit back and watch where Hunrath went, whom he spoke to, and what he did, and then try to reel in all the players—American and Russian—in one go. "Wait and see" was very much the name of the game.

While all of this was going on behind a thick veil of government secrecy, Wilkinson had got himself a job in Los Angeles with the Hoffman Radio Corporation—as head of the inspection department, no less. It was a good job, one which he had no desire to lose. In light of this, it's scarcely a surprise that Wilkinson became extremely worried about how his links to Hunrath might cause him trouble—and possibly even cause him to be fired from his new job. Wilkinson didn't exactly sever ties with his friend, but by 1953, he was content with Hunrath keeping him informed on what was going on in Saucer World, rather than playing a direct role in the subject.

Unfortunately for Wilkinson, he couldn't quite maintain that detached approach for too long: like a moth to a flame, he was soon back in the fold and back under the influence of Hunrath. Wilkinson's decision sealed his fate—and that of Hunrath, too—in ways scarcely imaginable.

Snatched from the Skies

November 10, 1953, was the date on which Hunrath and Wilkinson disappeared—never to be seen again. In the weeks leading up to their vanishing act, the two had allegedly contacted an extraterrestrial entity that, in essence, was downloading information into the minds of both men. George Hunt Williamson claimed to have personally seen this—late one night in his own Prescott, Arizona, home—and said it was downright eerie. It was, said Williamson, as if the pair, in almost complete darkness, was receiving messages from the great beyond, as one might when using a Ouija board. In one such session, in which Wilkinson and Hunrath almost appeared to be tripped out, said Williamson, they received directions that were destined to take them to a small airstrip near Gardena, Los Angeles County. The final curtain was about to come down on Hunrath and Wilkinson. According to Williamson, Hunrath and Wilkinson were soon to meet with aliens at a remote location in California—but where, exactly, he never knew.

On the morning of the day in question, the two men rented a car and headed to the airstrip. Why they didn't take one of their own cars, we don't know. Anticipation and excitement were rising quickly. Those levels increased as the airstrip finally came into view. Hunrath was a skilled pilot who had been flying for several years. They had rented a plane just a couple of days earlier and, on arrival at the airstrip, filled out the necessary paperwork; it was all going just fine. It failed to stay that way.

One of the staff recalled, later, that Hunrath had told him they were headed out to a specific area in the California desert, to meet with "friends." That same employee said that the plane had enough gas for about three hours of flight time and that the pair had planned to be back by late afternoon. He told the Feds there didn't seem to be anything unusual and that everything seemed in order. It was clearly *not* in order, though.

Wilkinson and Hunrath got in the plane and took to the skies, with that same employee looking on—at least, until he was sure all was good, which it seemed to be (*seemed* being the important word).

When, however, no further word was heard from either man by late afternoon—and with the staff at the airstrip getting panicky about their overdue plane and missing customers—the emergency services were called. After all, a missing aircraft was no small affair. Two missing men was even worse. Local pilots—chiefly, friends of the staff at the airstrip—offered to scour the area from above, and in just about every direction. No luck. No distress calls. No signs of billowing smoke or flames. No wreckage. There was nothing at all. Hunrath and Wilkinson had allegedly headed out to the desert and, in the process, had seemingly vanished into oblivion. Both the FBI and the local police dug into the matter. They too came up completely blank. Abducted from the skies? That was the rumor in the local UFO community. It's not at all surprising that the local media was soon on the trail of Hunrath and Wilkinson.

The Los Angeles Press Gets Involved

On November 20, ten days after the incident occurred, the *Los Angeles Mirror* ran a story on the missing men, the vanished plane, and the UFO connection. Since Hunrath was a bachelor, there was no one for the press to speak with. But it was a very different story when it came to Wilkinson. The media came knocking on the door of the Wilkinson home, looking to speak to Mrs. Wilkinson. Obviously concerned about the whereabouts of her husband—she didn't care too much at all for Hunrath—she agreed to have the story splashed across the pages of the newspaper, in the event that it might shed some light on things. It didn't. It just added to the mystery and the intrigue.

George Hunt Williamson, worried about the fate of his colleagues, followed the media's coverage of the story and noted the following to Frank Gibson:

Wilkinson's den was lined with flying saucer pictures, weird signs and formulas, which Mrs. Wilkinson said were supposed to be the new interplanetary language. "Of course, I don't quite go for all the Flying Saucer talk, but Karl convinced Wilbur they actually existed," said Mrs. Wilkinson. She then said, "Karl had tape recordings of conversations with men from other planets who landed here in Saucers." She showed reporters messages tacked on the wall of the den which were supposedly received by radio from the interplanetary visitors. One was from Regga of the planet Masar.

The search for Hunrath and Wilkinson went on for weeks, but with not a shred of luck. Despite careful checks in just about every direction (calls were even put in to both Mexican and Canadian authorities), not a single piece of data or physical evidence was ever found. They weren't just gone; they were *really* gone. Out there, so to speak. Eventually, and inevitably, the investigation came to an end. Mrs. Wilkinson and her children finally moved on with their lives. And no one else ever heard from those mysterious figures Mr. Bosco or Dr. Nagata again.

George Hunt Williamson, however, continued to look into the matter—he was, after all, one of the last people in the UFO research field to have seen Hunrath and Wilkinson before they vanished. Or were kidnapped. Williamson pondered the possibility that the two had flown to Mexico, but for what reason no one knew. There was no evidence that either man was involved in criminal activity. Plus, there were no problems with the Wilkinson's marriage.

Williamson added: "It has also been reported that Karl is in England and will reappear shortly and also that he has been seen recently in Los Angeles with his hair dyed! [Author's note: he did not reappear—ever.] He has been called a spaceman, a man possessed of evil spirits, an angel, a member of the FBI, and a Russian spy. What he really was no one knows—but we can guess."

We certainly can guess. Mrs. Wilkinson certainly did. She told the Los Angeles media something that got right to the heart of the conundrum: "I just can't help but think that flying saucers really had something to do with their disappearance."

A Bad Outcome for Karl Hunrath and Wilbur Wilkinson?

For us, for the FBI, and for the Wilkinson family, the story was over—albeit in completely unresolved fashion. But for Hunrath and Wilkinson, maybe it wasn't over. Perhaps they really were abducted by friendly alien creatures, maybe even living out the rest of their lives on a faraway, paradise-like world. Or perhaps their fates were far worse, which brings us to a 1962 episode of *The Twilight Zone,* "To Serve Man."

The story tells of a visit to Earth from a race of what appear to be benign extraterrestrials, the Kanamits. There is, quite naturally, some distrust on the part of world governments as to the motives of the aliens. So the United Nations gets involved, including one of its employees, Michael Chambers, a cryptographer. When a colleague of Chambers—Patty—decodes a large Kanamit book, she finds that its title is *To Serve Man.* This all sounds fine: the aliens are here to help us, after all. I should say that it all sounds fine until the final moments, when, as Chambers is about to board one of the Kanamit spacecraft, Patty finally decodes the *rest* of the book and screams: "Mr. Chambers, don't get on that ship! The rest of the book *To Serve Man,* it's . . . it's a cookbook!"

Food for thought. Or maybe, for Wilbur Wilkinson and Karl Hunrath, food for the aliens.

3 AN ABDUCTEE GOES TO "ANOTHER PLACE"

When it comes to weird and controversial alien abduction cases, it doesn't get more controversial or weird than that of a man named Antonio Villas Boas. He was a Brazilian man who, on October 5, 1957, had just about the closest encounter possible, as you will soon see. You'll also see what I mean by the term "the closest encounter possible." In all likelihood, the story would never have surfaced had it not been for a Dr. Olavo Fontes, who worked at the National School of Medicine in the Brazilian city of Rio de Janeiro. Before we get to the heart of the incident itself, it's important to note how, and under what circumstances, the story surfaced. As a result of his remarkable experience (which is putting things mildly), Villas Boas contacted a Brazilian journalist, Joao Martins—specifically because, although he was a regular writer for several newspapers, Martins also had a deep interest in UFOs and had written extensively about the subject for various Brazilian magazines and periodicals.

In the same way that Martins had a regular job but was heavily into the UFO issue, very much the same could be said for Dr. Fontes. He, too, was fascinated by the flying saucer phenomenon. Martins contacted Fontes in

1958—some months after Villas Boas's experience—on a different case, but in doing so, he happened to mention the Villas Boas affair just as an aside. Because of its profoundly unique nature, however, Fontes sat up and listened carefully. He did more than that: Fontes—as a result of his position in the medical field—agreed to not only interview Villas Boas but also run a series of tests on the man, which, history has shown, became part of an official medical file held in Fontes's office.

Since Villas Boas claimed various adverse physical side effects after the encounter, Fontes was able to utilize the science and medicine of a local hospital without cost to himself or to Villas Boas. This is why Fontes chose to present the case to the hospital as a medical one, rather than one which he would have to investigate privately and out of his own pocket. That same dossier also contained a statement made by Villas Boas which detailed his meeting with aliens. In other words, yes, Fontes had created the file as part of his duty as a doctor. But the file also had a positive role to play in relation to his UFO investigation. At the end of the day, though, it was a confidential medical file. It remained confidential until, with the permission of Villas Boas, Dr. Fontes, and the hospital, it was released into the public domain by Fontes in the early 1960s.

No Fewer Than Three Encounters

With the background to how the story surfaced in hand, let's now see what, precisely, happened to Antonio Villas Boas on the night of October 5, 1957. It's important to note the time frame in all of this: prior to the Villas Boas case, the vast majority of all the UFO incidents involving humanoid aliens were benign. One-to-one communications on a friendly wavelength were very much typical of what was reported—as we saw in Chapter 1, on the contactees. While the Villas Boas case did have an upside to it (one which Villas Boas found both exciting and satisfying), it was also noted for the fact that he was kidnapped under violent circumstances and manhandled. This was pretty much unheard of in the field of ufology. At least, in the early to mid-1950s. Now, we get to both the story and the, ahem, climax.

According to Villas Boas, he was captured by a group of extraterrestrials, taken on board their craft, and then made to have wild sex with a blisteringly hot babe from the depths of the universe. A close encounter? Hell, yes! Let's face it: it beats meeting an ET on the lawns of the White House or on a runway at Area 51. To see how the incident began, it's vital that we take a look at those now-declassified medical files, which were translated into English in the 1960s. With Dr. Fontes sitting opposite him, Villas Boas took a deep breath and told the story. And what a story it was.

"I live with my family on a farm which we own, near the town of Francisco de Sales, in the state of Minas Gerais, close to the border with the state of Sao Paulo," he began. It's a little-known fact that Villas Boas had *three* encounters. The first occurred more than a week before the main event. He explained to the doctor that he saw in the skies above the field he was working in "a very white light, and I don't know where it came from. It was as though it came from high up above, like the light of a car head-lamp shining downwards spreading its light all around . . . it finally went out and did not return."

Actually, it *did* return, a little less than a week later. Villas Boas was in the very same field, but this time his work was over and he was sitting on the family's tractor drinking something cold and refreshing. Then, that odd light of the previous week—or one of a similar nature—appeared on the scene. On this occasion, the craft got closer and closer, to the point that he could see the light was actually a structured vehicle. Villas Boas described it to Fontes as being "cartwheel"-like. It was, he estimated, around three hundred feet above the field. Clearly, the crew of the UFO was aware of Villas Boas's presence, as the object suddenly enveloped him with a deep red light. Curiously, the light irritated Villas Boas's eyes. It wasn't the brightness; it was something that had an adverse effect on his eyes themselves—something which made it into the official medical files on Villas Boas. Then, there was a definitive example of third time's the charm.

Immobilized and Abducted

In the very early hours of October 5, Villas Boas was still working around 1:00 a.m. when the night sky was yet again flooded with light. Back to the medical report: "At precisely 1:00 a.m., I suddenly saw a red star in the sky . . . In a few moments it had grown into a very luminous, egg-shaped object, flying towards me at a terrific speed. It was moving so fast that it was above the tractor before I had time to think what I should do."

It was all an amazed Villas Boas could do to stare in complete awe at the craft above him. That awe turned to cold fear when the vehicle descended to a height of maybe no more than seventy-five feet, at which point Villas Boas wisely thought his best course of action was to run like hell and get as far away from the whatever-it-was as possible. Unfortunately (or perhaps fortunately), it didn't quite work out like that.

Villas Boas describes what happened next: "It came nearer and nearer. I was now able to see it was a strange machine, rather rounded in shape, and surrounded by little purplish lights . . . [it] was like a large elongated egg with three metal spurs in front. . . . On the upper part of the machine there was something which was revolving at great speed and also giving off a powerful fluorescent reddish light." This description of the craft will become an integral—and even astonishing—part of the story later on.

Villas Boas, terrified, ran for his life. Or, to be precisely accurate, he *tried* to run for his life. No luck there. As a twenty-three-year-old, and someone who worked on a farm, he was fit and healthy and raced toward his family's farmhouse. He barely made it a couple hundred feet before he began to feel strange: his legs felt heavy, he was confused, dizziness swamped him, and in a few more seconds he was completely immobilized. He fell to the grass, on his back, and was just about able to make out a humanoid figure coming toward him. The figure was dressed in a one-piece outfit, not unlike those described by George Adamski and George Van Tassel in their encounters of a few years earlier. Villas Boas tried, again, to make a run for it, but it was no use. The being, and several more of its kind, grabbed Villas Boas and dragged him into the craft. Villas Boas had just been kidnapped by God knows what. And God knows what was going to happen next.

"I Did Not Feel Well"

What happened next was not what Villas Boas expected. He later admitted that he feared he was going to be kidnapped and never returned. Or worse, killed. As it happens, neither scenario was the correct one. When the four entities managed to haul Villas Boas aboard, he found himself in a very small room. There was barely enough room to swing a cat, never mind a creature from another galaxy. But Villas Boas wasn't in a position to swing anything, as he was still very much under the influence of whatever it was that had significantly and mysteriously incapacitated him. Then things got really strange.

In that small room, Villas Boas was stripped and covered head to foot in a sticky liquid. What it was, he was never told. The entities made an incision to his chin and extracted a small amount of blood, which was placed in a clear container. Villas Boas was then roughly forced into another small room. The door was locked, and Villas Boas was now on his own. In seconds, the room was filled with a noxious gas which affected his breathing. He recalled to Dr. Fontes, "It was as though I was breathing a thick smoke that was suffocating me, and it gave the effect of painted cloth burning. . . . I did not feel well and the nausea increased so much that I ended up vomiting."

Intriguingly, after his bout of sickness, Villas Boas suddenly felt much better. In fact, way better than he had felt in a very long time. That was good, as he was soon going to be ordered to make the performance of his lifetime.

Action Down Under

Still naked, and still in the same room, Villas Boas wondered who or what was coming next. It turned out that it was him. Suddenly, what looked like

31

a regular door, even down to the hinges, opened, and in walked another alien. This was not one of the black-eyed Greys. Nor was it one of George Adamski's Space Brothers. This was a slightly Asian-looking alien babe of major, curvy proportions and exotic appearance. And as naked as she was when she popped out of the womb. Villas Boas described her as follows:

Her hair was fair, almost white, smooth, not very abundant . . . her eyes were large and blue, more elongated than round, being slanted outwards . . . the cheekbones were very high . . . her lips were very thin, hardly visible . . . her body was much more beautiful than that of any woman I have ever known before. It was slim, with high and well-separated breasts, thin waist and small stomach, wide hips and large thighs . . . another thing that I noted was that her hair in the armpits and in another place was very red, almost the color of blood.

Do I really have to spell out what that other place was? You know the one: the one which our president bragged about grabbing when the mood took him and without permission. This was not what Villas Boas was expecting, but it was certainly what he got. Villas Boas, shocked and excited, stayed right where he was and was intent on letting the alien woman do the work. That is, until he suddenly felt like the cat that got the cream and took charge:

She came toward me silently, looking at me with the expression of someone wanting something, and she embraced me suddenly and began to rub her head from side to side against my face. I became uncontrollably excited, sexually, a thing that had never happened to me before. I ended up by forgetting everything, and I caught hold of the woman, responded to her caresses with other and greater caresses. Some of the grunts that I heard coming from that woman's mouth at certain moments nearly spoilt everything, giving the disagreeable impression that I was with an animal. Finally, she was tired and breathing rapidly. I was still keen, but she was now refusing, trying to escape, to avoid me, to finish with it all.

While Villas Boas said to Fontes that he could have done without all the grunting and growling, he was as proud as punch by his performance. With his ego still sky-high when he spoke to Fontes, Villas Boas opined, "That was what they wanted of me—a good stallion to improve their own stock."

The brief encounter of the interspecies type was over. Well, almost. There were two final, intriguing acts. Here's how Villas Boas described the first one: "She turned to me, pointed at her belly and then pointed toward me and with a smile she finally pointed towards the sky—I think it was in the direction of the south." The implication being that the woman was from the stars. The final thing was a quick tour of the craft, which is odd considering how badly Villas Boas was initially treated by his captors. He was then directed out of the craft and onto familiar ground. The vehicle took to the stars, his girlfriend from the galaxy presumably heading for new pastures and penises.

Villas Boas described the finale as follows:

The craft continued to rise slowly into the air until it had reached a height of some 30 to 50 meters. . . . The whirring noise of the air being displaced became much more intense and the revolving dish [that sat atop the object] began to turn at a fearful speed. . . . At that moment, the machine suddenly changed direction, with an abrupt movement, making a louder noise, a sort of "beat." Then, listing slightly to one side, that strange machine shot off like a bullet towards the south, at such a speed that it was gone from sight in a few seconds. Then I went back to my tractor. I left the craft at roughly 5.30 in the morning, having entered it at 1.15 in the early hours. So I had been there for four hours and fifteen minutes. A very long time indeed.

It was all over. The undeniably controversial and sensational nature of the story convinced Dr. Fontes to sit on it for a few years. In fact, when it reached the eyes and ears of 1960s-era ufology, most flying saucer researchers ignored it, poked fun at it, and suggested that perhaps Villas Boas wasn't the honest man that he seemed to be. For many flying saucer sleuths it was an embarrassing blot on the landscape, a blot they preferred to forget.

As the years passed, and as society became more open to the likes of what became known as "free love," ufology became more tolerant to controversial tales like that of Villas Boas. To the extent that by the 1970s, when more and more abductees were reporting sexual components to their experiences, such things were not frowned on or ignored: they were investigated deeply and seriously. The 1970s also brought forth a shocking and unforeseen development in the story of Villas Boas. It was a development which strongly suggested that Villas Boas was not abducted at all—at least, not by aliens. In that case, by whom? The answer to that question has a major bearing on the entire alien abduction controversy.

4 WHO ARE THE REAL ABDUCTORS?

Rich Reynolds has been on the UFO scene for many years—decades, actually. Refreshingly, Reynolds is someone who is not driven by Fox Mulder's "I want to believe" approach to ufology. Rather, he solely goes where the evidence and the facts take him. In February 1978—exactly twenty years after Antonio Villas Boas gave his statement to Dr. Olavo Fontes—Reynolds found himself immersed in the story.

It all began when Reynolds was approached by a mysterious, and perhaps even Machiavellian, character named Bosco Nedelcovic. He was born in Yugoslavia, but had moved to the United States decades earlier with his family. Nedelcovic carved quite a career for himself in the United States, working with the CIA and the Department of Defense, and securing a prominent position with the US Agency for International Development (AID). At least a part of his clandestine work in the 1960s was directed toward destabilizing prominent figures in the growing civil rights movement. There was also the matter of what Nedelcovic knew about the Antonio Villas Boas story.

Drugs and Mind Control

When Bosco Nedelcovic told Rich Reynolds what he—Nedelcovic—claimed was the truth behind the Villas Boas legend, Reynolds didn't know what to make of it. But he instantly realized that if what Nedelcovic was saying was true, it was destined to wreak havoc among the true believers in ufology. It's an established fact that at the very time Villas Boas was abducted, Nedelcovic *was* working for AID . . . *in South America*. Specifically in Brazil, which is where Villas Boas lived, worked, and encountered something incredible. According to Nedelcovic, Villas Boas was not abducted by aliens at all. Rather, Nedelcovic maintained that the entire event had been planned and executed by US intelligence—the CIA and several other agencies—and with additional help from AID. It was, Nedelcovic claimed, an operation that was born out of the CIA's notorious mind control program MK-Ultra, which began in the early 1950s. It was created to determine how the human mind could be altered and manipulated by hallucinogenic substances, psychedelics, and chemical cocktails, all designed to alter and control perception.

If the story told to Reynolds was nothing but a hoax or disinformation, it was certainly an intricate, well-thought-out tale, as the following demonstrates.

Seeking Out a Test Subject

Nedelcovic told Reynolds that late one evening in October 1957, his superior officer in AID told him to get to Aeroporto Santos Dumont—located in the heart of Rio de Janeiro—where a US Army–owned helicopter would be primed and ready to take him to destinations new. Puzzled by the fact that he had been told very little about the operation, Nedelcovic did as he was told and headed out to the airport. Sure enough, the large helicopter was ready and waiting when he arrived. Aboard it were several members of the US military, a few guys from AID, a doctor, and a senior officer in the Brazilian navy. They first headed out to a facility in the approximately

1,100 kilometers-long Espinhaço Mountains, staffed by both American and Brazilian military personnel. After a short period, the helicopter was airborne again, this time for Pico da Bandeira, the third tallest mountain in Brazil.

Nedelcovic said: "Various apparatus was tested during the flights but the three men from AID did not participate directly in the testing. They had been briefed on the mission and their function was outlined as auxiliary in nature. The briefing indicated that the men were participating in new forms of psychological testing that would eventually be used in military contexts."

About seventy-two hours later, the team was airborne again. After a brief trip back to the Espinhaço Mountains, it was time for the next part of the mission, which was to collect a wealth of technologies and contraptions, including what Reynolds called a "chrome-like Cubicle," which may well have been one of those compact rooms that a mind-warped Villas Boas recalled being pushed into. Further flights were made to collect various items for the mission, which had still not been clearly explained to Nedelcovic, although he would soon know the full story. It was on the next night, however, that the operation reached its peak: a young farmer was about to be used and manipulated in just about the strangest way possible.

Chased and Captured

It was while the helicopter crew made passes over various parts of Francisco de Sales—where Villas Boas lived at the time—that someone onboard saw a man on the ground, "a person below who had been discovered by heat-sensing devices on board." The unfortunate soul—who really was in the wrong place at the wrong time—was Villas Boas. The team had found what they had been ordered to find: a human guinea pig, in a remote area, who wouldn't be missed for a few hours. The helicopter pilot swooped low, spraying the area with what was described to Reynolds as "a chemical derivative" in gas form. The CIA had developed a specific agent which had the ability to alter perception and affect a person's ability to walk, run, or put up a fight—which sounds very much like the position that Villas Boas found himself in, as the "UFO" came close to him.

The pilot brought the helicopter to a careful landing, and a number of the team exited and raced toward the immobilized Villas Boas. In his weirded-out state, Villas was not in a position to do anything about it. Getting Villas Boas on board the helicopter proved to be a relatively simple task. The next step could have been tricky, but as fate would have it, it ran smoothly. Rich Reynolds told me, "The story from Nedelcovic was that after Villas Boas had been subjected to various drugs, the part with the woman was literally acted out. So, there may have been a real woman. But in Villas Boas's case, it could have been manipulation-induced. It gave me visions of the CIA employing people of an Asian kind of demeanor and look. It's in the realm of possibility that someone was concocting a scenario in that way."

Notably, the Freedom of Information Act has shown that in the 1950s and 1960s, the CIA used prostitutes in so-called "sting" operations. They were situations in which the agency needed information on a particular target—usually Russian. The hookers were used to place those same Russian targets in compromising sexual situations that were secretly filmed by CIA personnel, something all but guaranteed to convince the targets to talk or even defect. Remember how Villas Boas said the alien woman looked Asian? Intriguingly, some of those prostitutes employed by the CIA were Asian, too. In return for performing a sexual act in the name of national security, they would quietly be given a nice fee and residency in the United States. It was a deal which worked well for everyone—except, that is, for the targeted individual. In this case, Villas Boas.

When the operation was over, said Nedelcovic, a still-drowsy Villas Boas was carefully taken out of the helicopter and placed on the grass, next to his tractor. The helicopter then took to the skies for a final time, leaving a groggy Villas Boas to wonder what had just happened and what that strange thing in the sky really was.

Further Down the Rabbit Hole

If the revelations made by Bosco Nedelcovic to Rich Reynolds in February 1978 were the literal truth, then an important question most definitely requires answering: why would the US government, military, and intelligence community spend their time faking alien abductions? Rich Reynolds gave me an answer which may well get right to the crux of things. He said that while he is absolutely sure that a number of UFO cases reported in the early to mid-1950s were 100-percent bona fide, he suspects the US government didn't know what was going on, were unsure what the public should be told, and were concerned about how the public—whether on a local or worldwide scale—would react to the true UFO phenomenon. So they came up with a brainwave of a type that is undeniably mind-blowing.

Reynolds explained to me that after a series of very credible encounters with alien humanoids in France and Italy in the early 1950s, "the CIA didn't know how things might go from there, with the Italian and French cases and other ones, and how they should deal with it if there might have been an invasion. So, they set up people, like Villas Boas, in a UFO contrivance and studied the witness response, and probably studied the public and the media's response too."

We might also want to consider the distinct possibility that the sexual aspect of the Villas Boas incident was deliberately inserted to make the whole issue of alien abduction look ridiculous. To keep the press away from the subject—unless, that is, the media covered the controversy from a tongue-in-cheek perspective, which would have been perfectly fine for those in government who were secretly manipulating the abduction scene.

From a Flying Saucer to a Helicopter

For those who may still be doubtful of all this, take a look at Villas Boas's description of the UFO that he thought he saw, but which he probably did not. He said that the craft resembled "a large elongated egg" and that "[o]n the upper part of the machine there was something which was revolving at great speed and also giving off a powerful fluorescent reddish light." He added that the craft took to the skies slowly "until it had reached a height of some 30 to 50 meters. . . . The whirring noise of the air being displaced became much more intense and the revolving dish [that sat atop the object] began to turn at a fearful speed. . . . At that moment, the machine suddenly changed direction, with an abrupt movement, making a louder noise, a sort of 'beat.'"

The reference to the "revolving dish" atop the craft was, clearly, a description of the helicopter's rotor blades seen by a man whose mind was radically altered by an aerosol-based chemical agent. As for the "beating" noise, well, is there a better word to describe the classic sound of a helicopter? No, there is not.

So, what we have here is an incredible story, of equally incredible proportions that reveals something so amazing that it's practically unfathomable: there are *two kinds* of alien abductions. There are the all-too-genuine alien abductions, and then there are the US government's fabricated abductions. Both real, both terrifying to the witnesses, but both with radically different agendas. No wonder abductees find themselves in states of confusion, anxiety, and paranoia after their experiences—as did Antonio Villas Boas, for a short time. Although, in the long term it didn't affect him: he went on to become a respected attorney, who died in 1991 at the way too young age of fifty-six.

Two final things: It should be noted that AID—the agency for which Bosco Nedelcovic worked—states on its website that its primary role is to support "the foreign policy goals of the United States." Perhaps one of those foreign policy goals is to confuse overseas nations about the real nature of alien abduction.

And a question to ponder: were Bosco Nedelcovic and "Mr. Bosco," in the Karl Hunrath–Wilbur Wilkinson kidnapping-from-the-skies saga of 1953 one and the same? After all, Nedelcovic was Yugoslavian and Hunrath's Bosco had a noticeable European accent.

5 AN ALIEN ABDUCTION AND A "SPECIAL INTELLIGENCE"

Evidence of serious government concerns about the *real* alien abduction phenomenon continued into the 1950s, specifically in 1959. That was the year in which a young American soldier found himself caught up in a very strange saga that, to a degree, still disturbs him to this very day. It all went down on a chilly night in Utah's expansive desert. Private Bernard Gerry Irwin was the man whose life took a turn of the decidedly unforeseen type. February 20, 1959, began as a regular day for Irwin, but it most definitely didn't end that way. At the time, Irwin was driving to Fort Bliss, Texas, from Idaho—the former being the facility at which Irwin was stationed, and the latter his home state. As night set in, something completely unforeseen and paradigm-shifting happened to Irwin. He was about to be confronted by the UFO phenomenon in spectacular and mysterious fashion.

The night was dark, silent, and all but empty of vehicles, as desert highways so often are well after sunset. But for Irwin this was a night he would never forget—which is somewhat ironic, as a result of the fact that certain portions of his memory were forever erased from his mind. As he drove along the winding, curving road, Irwin was suddenly distracted by a bright light in the night sky—at a distinctly low level—that descended below a looming ridge. A meteorite? No. A flare, perhaps? Wrong again. Maybe an aircraft in trouble? That was Irwin's first thought, and with that in mind, he brought his car to a stop at the side of the road and turned on the blinkers. He quickly got out and left a note for passing drivers. It read: *Have gone to investigate what looks like a plane crash about one-quarter mile to my right. Notify state police immediately.* Wearing his army coat and armed with a flashlight, Irwin set off into the unknown. Irwin headed for what he suspected—and feared—just might be the site of a plane crash, only to find himself in an even greater nightmare.

Aliens and AWOL

The next thing Irwin remembered was waking up in a hospital bed in Cedar City, Utah. Where and why, he didn't know. A doctor and a nurse were standing around the bed, and they were soon joined by the county sheriff. Irwin was confused and scared, which is not surprising. The other three were far more interested in finding out what had gone on. Irwin kept muttering about "survivors," asking the nurse and the doctor if there were any. Were they all killed? Who "they" might have been, it seems no one really knew. That included Irwin, whose mind was in complete turmoil. The doctor then broke the news: Irwin had been unconscious for a full day and night. It was only thanks to a passing warden with the Fish and Game Commission, who came across Irwin's car, that Irwin was found. The police were soon on the scene, and Irwin was finally found, completely unresponsive, around a quarter mile from the road. It was in the early hours before Irwin was finally resting in an unfamiliar bed.

Irwin was kept under observation for several days but remained unable to recall any of the events of that strange night. Military personnel soon appeared on the scene to fly Irwin back to Fort Bliss, where he was placed under additional observation by a medical team. After about a full week, Irwin was declared back to full health. But try telling that to Irwin. Only a couple days after he got the green light to return to work, Irwin collapsed in a dead faint. When he came to, he failed to remember the names and faces of the people who had taken care of him on his return to his base.

Things got even weirder: in an almost-hypnotic state he got a bus ticket to Utah and headed out to the scene of the incident that had caused so much puzzlement and concern. In leaving his post, Irwin was officially AWOL—something that would come back to cause significant problems with his superior officers and later result in a fine and a loss of rank. In somewhat of a daze, Irwin then walked back to Cedar City. While Irwin was certainly in big trouble with his commanding officers, what's more intriguing was the response of the medical people who were required to continue to observe Irwin and try to figure out what had happened to him on that lonely, dark night.

An Intriguing Official File

Certainly, one of the most notable pieces of evidence that has surfaced via the Freedom of Information Act is a document prepared by a Captain Valentine, who was Irwin's psychiatrist while he was undergoing treatment for his strange condition. On March 27, 1959, Irwin was injected with sodium amytal. It provoked a strange response from Irwin, which caught Captain Valentine's deep attention. In his official report on this particular drug-induced session, the captain wrote the following:

[Irwin] stated there was a "special intelligence" that he couldn't explain to me, since it would be incomprehensible to me, which has directed him not to remember or not to tell me about any of the events in Utah. He says that if he tells what was behind the incidents in Utah there will be a "big investigation" that he does not want to be bothered with and also because it will harm many people and he doesn't want that to happen. He states "it" all began at the age of three years, although he will not reveal how or what began, stating that it would provide a clue to me as to what is behind all this. Also, he informed me that he could

leave this hospital any time if he wanted to by invoking a special force. Following this interview the patient stated he could remember nothing of what he said during it.

References to an Abduction?

Notably, David Booher—a UFO researcher who has carefully investigated the Irwin saga—has this to say regarding Irwin's statement made to Captain Valentine: "It's intriguing that Gerry speaks of an intelligence which 'directed him not to remember or not to tell me about any of the events in Utah.' As we know, in the decades that followed this would become a very common theme in the alien abduction literature, i.e. having memories blocked and/or being warned against telling others about the experience."

The Freedom of Information Act has also shown that the military, despite dosing Irwin with drugs to try to uncover the true story of that night in the desert in 1959, drew nothing but blanks. But the words of Captain Valentine strongly suggest he suspected that there was much more to the story than meets the eye—and particularly so considering that Irwin had alluded to the fact that something happened to him "at the age of three." It should be noted that alien abduction phenomena very often begins in early childhood.

The case of Private First Class Bernard G. Irwin is a most important one, as it set the scene for other cases and incidents to come. Things such as strange lights in the sky, and people being taken from their cars—or compelled to leave them—late at night, huge chunks of their memories gone. In some cases, but not all, gone forever. All of this now brings us to what is undeniably the veritable granddaddy of all abductions, and which has noticeable similarities to the experience that Gerry Irwin found himself in. It's time to take a trip back in time to 1961.

6 PLUCKED FROM THE ROAD

t's now time to turn our attention to what is, arguably, the most significant alien abduction account of all. Yes, there have been more extraordinary and amazing cases over the years, but the case in question has become a staple of ufological history, and for one particular reason: it was the first reported case of abduction that was taken seriously by UFO researchers. Yes, the Hunrath–Wilkinson affair of 1953 can be classed as a definitive abduction; but it's the case we're going to tackle now that contains all of the key ingredients of what it is that *really* defines an alien abduction.

The saga is also made notable by the fact that official files on the mysterious affair were created by the US military. And, as we'll see, there are good indications that the event galvanized the US Air Force into looking at the abduction phenomenon evermore closely and secretly—and what they found both shell-shocked and concerned the organization. It's a legendary story that took place on the night of September 19, 1961, and involved a married couple, Betty and Barney Hill, of New Hampshire.

The Drive of a Lifetime

On the night in question, Betty and Barney Hill were driving back from a vacation in Canada. The sky was black and filled with stars, the roads were winding, and a backdrop of huge mountains dominated much of the drive. A good time was had over the border and great memories were made: a visit to Niagara Falls was just one of the many highlights. Little did Betty and Barney know there was about to be another highlight—a deeply disturbing one. Indeed, it was filled with nothing but terror and trauma. As they negotiated the shadowy, dark roads on their return to New Hampshire, the Hills were about to encounter something unearthly and fear-filled. It was an event that was destined to radically alter and dictate the rest of their lives.

As the Hills got close to Lancaster, New Hampshire, at about ten thirty, they noticed something in the skies above them, and not at all far away. Whatever it was, the brightly lit vehicle was certainly no regular aircraft. Nor was it a helicopter. So, what was it? A sense of anxiety mixed with puzzlement and foreboding enveloped the pair—and in quick time, too. The Hills could only speculate on what *it* was—and to try to get a better view of it, too. Betty, already intrigued to the max by the presence of the futuristic-looking vehicle, suggested to Barney that he should pull the car over to the side of the road and grab his pair of binoculars, which he had taken with them on the vacation—which was most fortuitous, to say the very least. It was at a picnic area near Twin Mountain that Barney was able to stop the vehicle and see that whatever the object was, it definitely was no aircraft, even though it did have porthole-type windows that could be seen fairly clearly. Betty excitedly looked through the binoculars, as well—she too was convinced that the craft was definitely out of the ordinary, to put it mildly. The pair sat, almost in awe, as they concentrated on the mysterious craft that was already provoking thoughts in their minds of UFOs and alien creatures from a faraway world—maybe even a faraway galaxy. Adrenalin was pumping and tension was rising. Something was clearly going down, and the Hills were caught right in the middle of it. Not a good thing.

As they approached Franconia Notch, which is a pass in the vast White Mountain National Forest, the two got an even better look at the craft. It moved silently and effortlessly above giant firs, pines, and spruces. The Hills looked on, amazed, as the clearly rotating object performed all manner of astonishing maneuvers in the sky: it briefly hovered, then raced away at high speed, and finally returned to hang ominously in the air near their car. The pair continued to look on when two wings emerged from the sides of the craft, giving every impression that it was about to land. It turns out that their instincts were right on the money: creatures from another world were about to put in an appearance and turn the lives of the Hills upside down and inside out. A close encounter of the third kind? Undeniably.

Barney Goes for His Gun

Reaching Indian Head, the Hills continued to look on as the craft made a "swoop"-like movement and headed for the ground—and specifically for the Hills's car. Meanwhile, a strange buzzing sound emanated from the alien craft. In fact, the vehicle came so close that Barney feared for a few fraught moments that the object might even crash into them. As a result, he slammed on the brakes in the middle of the road, screeching to a halt. The wide-eyed pair watched as the object hovered over them at a height of about eighty feet—and like the veritable sword of mighty Damocles, himself.

Barney slowly opened the driver's side door, got out of the car in decidedly tentative fashion, and took out his pistol. His *loaded* pistol. You know, just in case. As he got closer, and with the benefit of the binoculars, Barney could see that there were a number of humanlike forms staring eerily back at him through the windows. Their eyes were penetrating, almost hypnotic, and they were all wearing black caps and black outfits. The sinister Men in Black who terrorize UFO witnesses? Not quite, but still a hell of a fear-filled sight on a dark night in the mountains. Then, something truly astonishing happened: Barney heard the voice of one of the aliens reverberating around his head. "Stay where you are and keep looking," was the mind-to-mind order. Barney did as he was told in fear of what might happen if he tried to do something reckless, like maybe take a potshot at the craft with his pistol. Concerned that the aliens were about to "capture" him and Betty—and maybe even their beloved dog, Delsey, who had also had a good time in Canada—Barney raced back to the car, fired up the engine, and hit the road at high speed. Neither Betty nor Barney wanted to end up in an alien zoo. Or, worse still, on an extraterrestrial dinner plate. Thankfully, the craft soon vanished and the Hills were able to finally take a few deep breaths. Barney eased off the pedal and Betty began to relax. Only Delsey was blissfully unaware of the momentous event.

Nightmares and Erased Hours

As they continued on with their journey, and as they got their wits about them, both husband and wife speculated about what on earth—or off it—they had encountered in the heavens above. There was very little they could do other than class it as a definitive UFO. They were understandably excited, but disturbed, too, and for reasons they couldn't quite grasp. It was in the days and weeks ahead, however, that something nerve-jangling happened—something which finally led them to uncover the truth of the encounter. Barney and Betty began to experience terrifying nightmares, both of an eerily similar nature and quite out of the blue.

In the dreams, the UFO did *not* swoop away, but actually landed not far from them, and the crew proceeded to take the almost-mind-controlled pair onto their ship. It was then that the worst part of the encounter reared its ugly head. Both were placed on tables, and strange experiments were quickly begun: Betty had a device inserted into her navel by the aliens—and for reasons that remain baffling to this very day. Barney was made to ejaculate. The inference was clear: the extraterrestrials were engaged in a strange and clandestine program that was somehow directly connected to the issue of human reproduction. And the Hills were the victims of beings from another world.

Not only that, but upon getting home the Hills realized that several hours could not be accounted for: the journey had somehow taken longer than it should have. Something happened on the drive that had been wiped from their memories, but which was still buried deep in their minds—and to the extent that fragments of it were starting to surface in their dream states. That wasn't all. The strap on Barney's binoculars was inexplicably torn. His shoes were torn, too. Betty's dress that she had worn on the trip back was ripped. And the watches of both Betty and Barney never again worked properly. Clearly, there was much more to the story, but whatever it was, the Hills were unable to fully remember.

There most definitely was much more to the story; more than both Betty and Barney could ever have imagined in the immediate days after their experience. It was all suggestive of the probability that the Hills had been taken on board a spacecraft from another world and subjected to trauma-filled experiments of a very bizarre nature. For the strange and enigmatic creatures that kidnapped the pair and almost completely erased their memories, Betty and Barney were nothing but the human equivalent of lab rats—although the Hills would not realize this immediately.

Incredibly, the two endured this stress-filled situation for about two years. Finally, though, as 1963 came to its end, and as the nightmares became too much for Barney and Betty, they decided to seek help. Enough was now most certainly enough. They got the help they needed in the form of a man named Benjamin Simon, who was a Boston-based psychiatrist skilled in the field of hypnosis. The way and means by which the Hills and Simon came together was strange indeed—almost as if it were planned by the hand of fate itself.

A Fortuitous Meeting

On November 22, 1963—the day on which President John F. Kennedy lost his life, in Dealey Plaza, Dallas, Texas—Betty and Barney went to their church, where the speaker was a man named Ben H. Swett, a published poet. He shared his writings with the audience—which included the Hills. Swett had another skill, too: he was a captain in the US Air Force and ultimately rose to the rank of a full colonel, retiring in 1985. Not only that, Swett, who was stationed at the time at Pease Air Force Base, New Hampshire, had a deep interest in hypnosis. Learning this, Barney cautiously told Captain Swett of the strange events of that September 19 night in the mountains. Swett exhibited a great deal of interest in the story, particularly the part concerning the peculiar time lapse. Swett thanked the pair for sharing their story and hit the road. Just under a year later, though, he was back.

In September 1963, Captain Swett gave a second presentation to the churchgoers. On this occasion, though, poetry wasn't on the agenda. But hypnosis was. The captain gave a detailed history of hypnosis to the congregation, and Barney and Betty were captivated by what Swett had to say. They quickly realized that hypnosis just might open more than a few doors, behind which lay the truth about whatever really happened to them back in 1961. Barney was already seeing a psychiatrist, a Dr. Duncan Stevens. This was as a result of the trauma caused by the encounter, which had led to a number of ailments exacerbated by stress, including a serious stomach ulcer. So, Captain Swett suggested that Barney should bring up the issue of hypnosis with Dr. Stevens—which he did. It was Stevens who pointed the Hills in the direction of Dr. Benjamin Simon.

An Interrupted Journey and a Book

When he heard the story from Betty and Barney, Dr. Simon realized that there was far more to the affair than the pair could recall consciously: just about everything was buried within their subconscious. It was now time to dig deep and haul out those memories. Which is exactly what happened.

Benjamin Simon knew all too well that the complex nature of the human brain could cause people to blot out fear-filled events. In the case of the Hills, though, it seemed that something else was afoot too: namely, that Betty and Barney's memories had been *deliberately* wiped clean—or at least to the point where they didn't have full, conscious recall of what had happened to them but still retained vague memories of that fateful night and while in the dream state. As Simon continued to work with the couple, what surfaced was a tale of full-blown alien abduction, missing time, and distressing experiments—all orchestrated by strange-looking humanoid entities from an unknown world.

Such was the interest in the story, when it became public—partly due to the fact that the Hills began giving public lectures on their encounter—that writer John Fuller penned a full-length book on the tale. It was published in 1966 and with the permission of both Betty and Barney. It had a very apt title: *The Interrupted Journey*. The book became a huge hit with not just the UFO research community but the public too. Even the mainstream media covered the tale—and not always in a fun-poking fashion. The old days of the long-haired, largely friendly Space Brothers of the 1950s were gone. The early 1960s had given rise to a new breed of ET: a band of seemingly emotionless, drone-like beings who saw us as nothing more or less than animals ripe for their strange and even sinister experimentation.

There is, however, another aspect to all of this; one driven by, and saturated in, secrecy and conspiracy. It's time now to take a look at what the US government knows about Betty and Barney Hill.

The US Military Gets Involved

Although Betty and Barney did not seek professional help for their nightmares until 1963, just a few days after their encounter they shared the details they could remember with a man who was a good friend of Barney. His name was James MacDonald. More correctly, Major James MacDonald, USAF, Retired. It turns out that MacDonald also did clandestine work with none other than the CIA. Betty Hill's niece, Kathleen Marden, says of this curious affair, "[Macdonald's] tie to the intelligence community has led to speculation among researchers that his presence at the meeting was more than social." Betty rejected this theory, but it is worth noting.

It was also just a couple of days after their close encounter that Betty contacted staff at Pease Air Force Base—where Captain Swett happened to be stationed. It was no secret at the time that the Air Force—via its UFO investigation program, Project Blue Book—investigated UFO sightings. So Betty felt that the responsible thing to do was to let the staff know, in case they found the story interesting. They did. And way more, too. Betty made a call to the base and was transferred to a military officer, who took notes on what Betty had to say. Evidently, the Hills's experiences caught the attention of someone, because later on that very same day the phone rang. Betty said, "Hello" and found herself speaking with a Major Paul W. Henderson. Betty was pleased that someone was listening and told the whole story—or at least the parts of the story she consciously recalled. Major Henderson was particularly intrigued by what Betty had to say—to the point where he called back the next day. The result was that Major Henderson prepared a detailed report on the mysterious affair.

(SECURITY INFORMATION when filled in)

SUPPLEMENT TO AF FORM 112

CLASSIFICATION					
ORIGINATING AGENCY	REPORT NO.		PAGE	OF	PAGES
100th Bomb Wing (M) SAC (DCOI)	100-1-61		3	3	

object. They continued on their trip and when they arrived in the vicinity of Ashland, N.H., about 30 miles from Lincoln, they again heard the "buzzing" sound of the "object"; however, they did not see it at this time.

Mrs Hill reported the flight pattern of the "object" to be erratic, changed directions rapidly, that during its flight it ascended and descended numerous times very rapidly. Its flight was described as jerky and not smooth.

Mr. Hill is a Civil Service employee in the Boston Post Office and doesn't possess any technical or scientific training. Neither does his wife.

During a later conversation with Mr. Hill, he volunteered the observation that he did not originally intend to report this incident but in as much as he & his wife did in fact see this occurence he decided to report it. He says that on looking back he feels that the whole thing is incredible and he feels somewhat foolish - he just can not believe that such a thing could or did happen. He says, on the other hand, that they both saw what they reported and this fact gives it some degree of reality.

Information contained herein was collected by means of telephone conversation between the observers and the preparing individual. The reliability of the observer cannot be judged and while his apparent honesty and seriousness appears to be valid it cannot be judged at this time.

A US Air Force document on the September 1961 abduction of Betty and Barney Hill (courtesy of the US Air Force)

Betty herself stated, "Major Henderson asked to speak with Barney, who was hesitating about talking on the phone. But, once he was on the phone, he was giving more information than I had. Later, Barney said he had done this, for Major Henderson did not seem to express any surprise or disbelief."

It's worth reading the document in its entirety, as it may well be the very first official military report on a UFO encounter in which the primary witnesses were abducted by nonhuman creatures. Of course, we cannot say for sure that the military did not have pre-existing, secret knowledge of the abduction phenomenon—and, admittedly, the 1959 abduction of Gerry Irwin points in that direction, as does the Hunrath–Wilkinson saga—but, the Henderson document is significant as it's the earliest officially released document on alien abductions.

Creating a Real X-File on Betty and Barney

In his report, Major Henderson wrote the following, which adds important little-known facts to the story:

On the night of 19–20 September between 20/0001 and 20/0100 the observers were traveling by car in a southerly direction on Route 3 south of Lincoln, N.H., when they noticed a brightly lighted object ahead of their car at an angle of elevation of approximately 45 degrees. It appeared strange to them because of its shape and the intensity of its lights compared to the stars in the sky. Weather and sky were clear. They continued to observe the moving object from their moving car for a few minutes, then stopped. After stopping the car they used binoculars at times.

They report that the object was traveling north very fast. They report it changed directions rather abruptly and then headed south. Shortly thereafter, it stopped and hovered in the air. There was no sound evident up to this time. Both observers used the binoculars at this point.

While hovering, objects began to appear from the body of the "object," which they describe as looking like wings, which made a

V-shape when extended. The "wings" had red lights on the tips. At this point they observed it to appear to swoop down in the general direction of their auto. The object continued to descend until it appeared to be only a matter of "hundreds of feet" above their car.

At this point they decided to get out of that area, and fast. Mr. Hill was driving, and Mrs. Hill watched the object by sticking her head out the window. It departed in a generally northwesterly direction, but Mrs. Hill was prevented from observing its full departure by her position in the car.

They report that while the object was above them after it had "swooped down" they heard a series of short, loud "buzzes," which they described as sounding like someone had dropped a tuning fork. They report that they could feel these buzzing sounds in their auto. No further visual observation was made of this object. They continued on their trip and when they arrived in the vicinity of Ashland, N.H., about 30 miles from Lincoln, they again heard the "buzzing" sound of the "object"; however, they did not see it at this time.

Mrs. Hill reported the flight pattern of the "object" to be erratic; [it] changed directions rapidly, [and] during its flight it ascended and descended numerous times very rapidly. Its flight was described as jerky and not smooth. Mr. Hill is a civil service employee in the Boston Post Office and doesn't possess any technical or scientific training. Neither does his wife.

During a later conversation with Mr. Hill, he volunteered the observation that he did not originally intend to report the incident but in as much as he and his wife did in fact see this occurrence he decided to report it. He says that on looking back he feels that the whole thing is incredible and he feels somewhat foolish—he just cannot believe that such a thing could or did happen. He says, on the other hand, that they both saw what they reported, and this fact gives it some degree of reality.

Information contained herein was collected by means of telephone conversation between the observers and the preparing individual. The reliability of the observer cannot be judged, and while his apparent honesty and seriousness appears to be valid, it cannot be judged at this time.

The file does not end there. Rather intriguingly, only hours after the Hills's encounter, staff at Pease Air Force Base tracked the movements of an anomalous target in nearby skies. Once again, it was down to Major Henderson to record the facts of the strange incident, which occurred around two in the morning:

During a casual conversation on 22 Sept 61 between Major Gardiner D. Reynolds, 100th BW DCOI and Captain Robert O. Daughaday, Commander 1917-2 AACS DIT, Pease AFB, NH it was revealed that a strange incident occurred at 0214 local on 20 Sept. No importance was attached to the incident at that time. Subsequent interrogation failed to bring out any information in addition to the extract of the Daily Report of the Controller. It is not possible to determine any relationship between these two observations, as the radar observation provides no description. Time and distance between the events could hint of a possible relationship [italics mine].

Major Henderson also recorded the logbook entry of the Daily Controller at Pease AFB: "Observed unidentified A/C come on PAR 4 miles out. A/C made approach and pulled up at ½ mile. Shortly after observed weak target on downwind, then Clutter Time Constant radar lost. Tower was advised of A/C when it was on final, then when it made low approach. Tower unable to see any A/C at any time."

And things are still not over.

Someone Else Takes an Interest

It's very intriguing to note that it was not just Major Henderson who was exhibiting interest in the Hill saga—other government parties were too. In Betty's very own words, "Later, Major Henderson called back and asked if we would be willing to *be put through to somewhere else, and have our calls monitored.* We agreed to this. One call was transferred to another place and *today we do not know with whom we were talking* [italics mine]."

It may be speculation, but it could be said that the "somewhere else" to which Betty referred was an office that was taking careful and secret notice of the alien abduction phenomenon—and ensuring that they had secured all of the much-needed data on the case. This thought-provoking theory is given even more credence by the fact that only months after the experience of Betty and Barney Hill, British military authorities quietly and carefully began investigating cases extremely similar to that of Betty and Barney. Classified not just for years, but for *decades*, some of those files have now begun to surface, thanks to the terms of the UK's Freedom of Information Act. The stories they tell are amazing and incredible, as will be demonstrated in the following two chapters.

As for Betty and Barney Hill, their lives went in very different directions. Yes, they remained a devoted, loving couple. But Barney was never able to shed the trauma and stress that had overwhelmed him as a result of that mysterious night in September 1961. His ulcer worsened, and in 1969 he died at the tragically early age of forty-six from a cerebral hemorrhage, just a couple of months after ever-faithful Delsey the dog passed away. Betty was now alone. She soon embraced the UFO subject to a greater degree, however, and became an undeniable celebrity in those places where UFO enthusiasts congregate. Betty remained active in ufology for decades, passing away in 2004. She was eighty-five.

7 MEANWHILE, ON THE OTHER SIDE OF THE POND . . .

Just five months after Betty and Barney Hill's late-night encounter, a similar incident occurred in the United Kingdom. In this case, the witness was a man named Ronald Wildman. It was in the early hours of February 9, 1962, that Wildman had an extraordinary experience, one which led him to fully believe he had seen a UFO at very close quarters. Amazed and slightly unsettled by what had occurred, Wildman contacted the local police, who later shared his story with the United Kingdom's Air Ministry, which is today called the Ministry of Defense (MoD). The press, tipped off by the police, gave the story more than a bit of coverage, which led the UKs UFO research community to descend on Wildman and pick his brain about what he saw, too.

Behind the scenes, the military was maintaining a very close watch of Wildman and his experience. That much can be proved: the old Air Ministry file on the man and his encounter has been released into the public domain and can be accessed in person at the National Archives in Kew, England. The Wildman file runs from 1962 to 1964 and is predominantly comprised of clippings taken from newspapers, various issues of *Flying Saucer Review* magazine—a popular publication for UFO enthusiasts, particularly in the 1960s and 1970s—and other newsletters and journals covering the issue of flying saucers. The file contains something else too, as you will now learn.

Exactly one week after the furor concerning Ronald Wildman's encounter calmed down, an employee of the British Royal Air Force (RAF) Provost and Security Services (P&SS) paid a quiet visit to the local police to get all the data they had in hand. It should be noted that the P&SS is an elite arm of RAF. Its employees typically get involved in the investigation of terrorist threats against the military. They are experts in disinformation and espionage, and are skilled in counterintelligence. That the Air Ministry felt it was important for Wildman's case to be investigated by the P&SS speaks volumes for its credibility. With that all said, let's take a look at the initial report prepared by P&SS officer Sergeant C.J. Perry:

At Aylesbury on 16th February 1962, at 1530 hrs., I visited the Civil Police and requested information on an alleged "Flying Saucer" incident. I was afforded every facility by the Civil Police authorities and although no official report had been made, details of the incident were recorded in the Station Occurrence book. The details are as follows:

Mr. Ronald Wildman of Luton, a car collection driver, was traveling along the Aston Clinton road at about 0330 hrs. on 9th February 1962 when he came upon an object like a hovercraft flying approximately 30 feet above the road surface. As he approached he was traveling at 40 mph but an unknown force slowed him down to 20 mph over a distance of 400 yrd., then the object suddenly flew off.

Perry goes on to describe the object as being about forty feet wide and oval in shape with a number of small portholes around the bottom edge. It reportedly emitted a fluorescent glow but was otherwise not illuminated. Wildman reported the incident to a police patrol, who notified the duty sergeant, Sergeant Schofield. A radio patrol car was dispatched to the area, but no further trace of the "Flying Saucer" was seen. It was the opinion of the local police that the report by Wildman was genuine and the experience was not a figment of imagination. They saw that he was obviously shaken.

I spoke to Sergeant Schofield and one of the constables to whom the incident was reported. Both were convinced that Ronald Wildman was genuinely upset by his experience.

The Missing Time Phenomenon Surfaces Again

As interesting as the above account certainly is, a follow-up report from Sergeant Perry reveals something more. It's presented only as a passing reference, but—from the perspective of the story you are reading—it is incredibly important. Following a return visit to see Sergeant Schofield, Sergeant Perry wrote in his report that the police had failed to mention one particular thing in the initial discussion. At the time, the police didn't feel it was too important. Namely, when he spoke with the police, Ronald Wildman was "muddled about the time." Regrettably, these four words are not expanded on, but as brief as they are, they suggest there was some degree of missing hours—that Wildman believed the time frame of the encounter was very different to what it *really* was.

There is one more important factor in this story: copies of Sergeant Schofield's report on the Wildman incident were copied to a division of the Air Ministry called A.I. (Tech) 5(b). The "A.I." stands for "Air Intelligence." Many years ago, A.I. (Tech) 5(b) was absorbed into MoD's Defense Intelligence staff. For a case that involved a man whose car was briefly affected by a close encounter with a UFO, this is an extraordinary high degree of interest—all displayed by covert branches of UK military and intelligence services.

It's not at all impossible that US authorities—carefully watching the growing abduction phenomenon in the United States—may well have confided in their British cousins the details of the 1961 experiences of Betty and Barney Hill. Maybe even the 1959 encounter of Gerry Irwin. After all, the United States and the Brits have, for decades, had a good, solid working relationship when it comes to matters relative to mutual national security.

It would have made a great deal of sense—when faced with the startling realization that US citizens were being kidnapped by extraterrestrial creatures—for the Americans to have warned the British government of this expanding threat. Probably, that's exactly what happened. And, maybe, it's for that reason that the Ronald Wildman incident was treated so seriously and handled by the elite of the British Royal Air Force.

Another Encounter and Another Visit by the Authorities

Six months after the Ronald Wildman issue, there was another incident—or, rather, incidents—that caught the attention of the P&SS. Before we get to the case itself, however, it's important to note that in many incidents of alien abduction, the events revolve around young girls who are woken up in the early hours of the morning and who see strange lights outside of their bedroom windows—as if almost beckoning them to come for a closer look. From that point onward, the girl is taken from her home and a full-blown experience/abduction quickly follows. Notably, the case that follows concerns none other than a young girl who had her very own strange, bedroom-based encounters. It's even more notable that the P&SS were quick to speak to the witness. They were also careful to ensure that she kept quiet about what exactly she encountered.

From Sleep to Unearthly Visitor

It was late August 1962: Marilyn Monroe had died under controversial circumstances just a few weeks earlier. And US intelligence began to suspect that the Soviets were secretly transferring nuclear weapons to Cuba—something that, two months later, brought the world to the brink of nuclear war. For a young girl named Anne Leamon, though, life went on as it always had. Just sixteen at the time of her encounter, Anne lived on a farm run by her family in the English county of Somerset. It was a picturesque area: Anne's bedroom backed right onto the green and inviting Brendon Hills, which today are part of the huge Exmoor National Park.

As the released documents on Anne's encounter reveal, she woke up late one evening—for no particular reason she could fathom—and looked straight out of one of the windows. She was confronted by the sight of a circular light hovering over the hills. It was also changing color: from red to green and then to yellow. Strange rays of light emanated from the source. Anne looked on, utterly transfixed. Quite naturally, her first assumption was that it had to be a star, although she had never seen a star like this before. It became very apparent the object was no star when it suddenly began to move. She considered that it might have been a helicopter, but that theory was dismissed as a result of the overwhelming silence.

Suddenly, the object came toward Anne, and in her own words, she felt "attracted" to it. Almost mesmerized by its flickering lights and rapidly changing colors. It then reversed, moved sideways, and then headed back to the hills. It was as if the display was meant for Anne herself, which was likely the case. For around an hour, the light kept its position above the hilly countryside; then it finally shot away and vanished. This was not the end of things, however. There was far more to come.

The UFO Returns, and Anne Leamon Gets a Visitor

Anne had an eerie feeling that the light would return to her the following night. It did—but this time, it was well into the early morning hours. Yet again, it glided across the Brendon Hills, stopping outsider her bedroom window. She admitted to becoming "quite friendly" with the light, which she felt was not in any way dangerous, even though she was mystified by its origin and intent. Anne took a very proactive approach and made drawings of the object, even tracking its movements via a compass. And the light came again and again—always well into the early hours of the morning and always approaching Anne's bedroom.

Puzzled but intrigued by her stranger in the night, Anne decided to do something that would ultimately lead to a secret file being opened on her—one which was classified for thirty years. She telephoned a military facility to report what she had seen: Royal Marines Base Chivenor, as it is known today. To this day, the facility remains a vital component of the British government's defense network.

As interesting as the late-night light displays were for Anne, she hardly expected that a senior official in the military would visit her home and interview her at length. After all, it wasn't as if she was reporting the landing of a UFO, or talking about a face-to-face encounter with bug-eyed aliens. But that's exactly what happened: Anne *was* visited, and she became the subject of a large file that commanded the attention of a covert arm of the military. It's a file now in the public domain at the National Archives.

It was late one evening when there was a knock at the front door. Anne's mother opened it and was confronted by a man dressed in a black suit who had arrived in a black car. He identified himself as a Sergeant J.W. Scott of the Provost and Security Services—the very same unit that investigated the Ronald Wildman case in February 1962, a case that had also occurred well after midnight. Had Anne and her family had good knowledge of the UFO subject at the time, they would surely have believed they were in the presence of one of the dreaded MIB. In a sense, that's what he was.

A Suggestion Not to Talk

So determined was Sergeant Scott to see the mysterious light that he visited the Leamon home on at least three occasions, sitting patiently and near silently in Anne's bedroom with her and keeping a careful lookout for the object. It was on the third occasion that Sergeant Scott finally saw the UFO—for that is surely what it was: an unidentified light-form in the skies above. Notably, Anne stated that Sergeant Scott quickly grabbed the camera he had brought with him, leaned through the window, and took several photos. The mysterious object was now captured—at least on film. Anne noted that Scott seemed to deliberately try to play down the matter and did his utmost to avoid sensationalizing what Anne thought was a very exciting development in the matter. For Anne, though, it was practically impossible for her *not* to be excited: after all, a member of a covert arm of the UK military was standing in her bedroom, firing off photo after photo of an aerial visitor of the very weird variety.

When the object vanished from view, Sergeant Scott got ready to leave; his air of calmness still completely intact: he wasn't giving away anything. But he did take something with him: Anne's drawings and compass notes. Despite promising to return them, Scott never did. He vanished into the night—with all of the available data and documentation—never to be seen again. Before vanishing, though, Scott did suggest to Anne that it would not be a good idea to share the story of her experiences with her school friends—or, indeed, with anyone else at all, including the media.

Anne was mystified by the whole thing. Even more so when, several weeks later, she got a response from the Air Ministry saying that she had seen nothing stranger than a star. Does it really require an operative of the Provost and Security Services—the "007s" of the Royal Air Force—to spend so much time and effort looking into the movements of a star? One would imagine they had far better things to do with their time, particularly given the fraught, ongoing situation with the Russians and Fidel Castro's regime in Cuba. It must be said that one of the things which attracted Anne to the object was its movement: it shot around the sky, even coming close to her bedroom window on several occasions. Stars, I probably don't need to tell you, certainly do not act in such a fashion. Nor do planets. Nor do aircraft or helicopters, either.

We can learn a great deal from this undeniably weird series of events. A young girl has close encounters in the dead of night and in her bedroom, which mirrors the ways in which numerous alien abduction encounters begin. She is soon visited by a Man in Black who spends *three nights* with her, catches the object on film, grabs her drawings, and leaves her home with a "friendly warning" not to talk about what she had seen. All of this for a star? Not a chance.

Now, we'll see a *third* example of how and why the Provost and Security Services got involved in yet another late-night encounter with a UFO— which also just happens to have occurred late at night. And it, too, involved a young woman. For the P&SS, a pattern was developing. It wasn't a good pattern.

8 ALIEN ENCOUNTER AT AN OLD BRIDGE

For further evidence of how, in the 1960s, the British military was secretly opening files on those citizens of the United Kingdom who were suspected of being abductees, we have to focus on the intriguingly weird story of a young woman named Diane Foulkes. The year was 1966; the month was November. It was a month in which NASA's Lunar Orbiter 2 was launched, John Lennon met Yoko Ono for the first time, and Ronald Reagan was elected governor of California. Those historic events all paled against what Diane Foulkes had to endure: a close encounter with a strange craft in the sky and a period of missing time. As the United Kingdom's Freedom of Information Act has shown, it was our old friends, the Royal Air Force's Provost and Security Services, who secretly oversaw the investigation into Diane's trauma-dominated experiences.

We would almost certainly be completely oblivious to the facts of the affair today were it not for one significant thing: Diane Foulkes's family decided to contact the military in an effort to try to understand the nature of her experiences. At the time, twenty-two-year-old Diane—a typist working at a local company—was living with her parents in the old English town of Shrewsbury, in the county of Shropshire. It's a town which was founded way back in the ninth century, and its ancient architecture would not at all look out of place on the likes of *Downton Abbey*—nor would its surrounding green fields and hills, little old villages, and expansive woods.

As for Diane's encounter with something definitively unknown, it occurred on the night of November 8, 1966. Although she kept silent on what had happened for two days, she finally confided in her mother and father on the tenth, revealing all. So shocked were Diane's parents by what she had to say that her mother promptly contacted the local military base, Royal Air Force (RAF) Shawbury, which was constructed in the later stages of the First World War and that, today, is a training facility for military helicopter pilots. She spoke to a Flight Lieutenant Williams, who took a few notes and promised to pass the data on to the right people. We will soon learn who they were.

We'll likely never know what was going through the mind of Diane's mother when she made that call to RAF Shawbury, but one can imagine it would not have been the easiest of things to do. After all, she was about to share the details of her daughter's encounter with what may well have been a spacecraft constructed on another world. If Diane had worries about what the authorities might say, she had no need to. It's most intriguing to note that the military took her story very seriously. To the extent that, four days later, a three-man team arrived at the Foulkes's home. Questions were about to be asked, and a secret file was about to be created.

"The Object Had Kept Pace with Her"

It was about seven in the evening when the knock on the door—which Diane Foulkes may have been dreading or looking forward to—finally came. Diane herself opened it and was confronted by three men dressed in plainclothes. The man who knocked on the door identified himself as Corporal Robert A. Rickwood of the Royal Air Force. Notably, Corporal Rickwood carefully avoided adding that he also happened to be attached to the P&SS Special Investigation Section, SIS, which undertook investigations of events with national security implications. Diane invited the three men into the living room. They sat down, while her parents hovered awkwardly in the background. In typical English fashion, tea was made for everyone, and the interview began.

Corporal Rickwood, perhaps aware that Diane was somewhat nervous, simply asked her to relate the facts, and added that he was there to help and try to figure out what it was that she had seen just a few nights earlier. Diane took a deep breath and began. She had been out for an evening with friends, and with midnight barely five minutes away, she was approaching the little village of Great Ness, which even today has a population of fewer than one thousand. Then something weird happened, something totally unforeseen: Diane had an encounter of the UFO type. As a quick aside, Diane said that this was not her first encounter of this particular type. She had had another close encounter—late at night, and in the same area— two years earlier. This was, of course, a surprise to Corporal Rickwood's team. As a result, he suggested that Diane go back to the beginning, to ensure that they had all of the data in hand and in chronological order. An incredible tale was about to unfold.

Corporal Rickwood's now declassified report states, in part, the following:

The first occurred two years ago in November 1964, when she had been driving from Shrewsbury to her home along the A5 road. This was at about 0200 hours as she neared the Montford Bridge over the River Severn. Approximately midway between Shrewsbury and Great Ness a brightly lit circular object appeared in the sky above her car.

She had been frightened and had accelerated along the road. The object had kept pace with her remaining at the same height until she arrived home. She had told her mother and father who also watched the object. She described the object as an especially bright light in the sky which remained stationary due west from their home for about half an hour. It had then rapidly diminished in size and they assumed it had accelerated away from them. No sound was heard from the object.

The light was yellow in color and became red as it diminished.

As fascinating as all of this certainly is, it was yet another aside from Diane which had the P&SS guys sitting up and really taking notice. According to Diane, there was a lapse in time: although it was about two in the morning when she reached the Montford Bridge, it should actually have been much closer to one. If Corporal Rickwood and his colleagues knew that this was highly suggestive of an abduction experience, they did not make a comment to this effect, which is hardly surprising. The last thing they would have wanted to do would be to plant thoughts in Diane's mind suggesting that she had been kidnapped by aliens, and that certain memories of the event had been obliterated. They wanted her calm and focused. It was now time for Diane to reveal what she encountered just four nights before Corporal Rickwood paid a visit. Let's see what the corporal recorded next, in his secret report:

The second incident occurred on the 8th November 1966 at 2355 hours and again whilst she was returning from Shrewsbury on the same road. The object had again appeared at Montford Bridge, but this time it was much lower in the sky and on the north side of the road. On this occasion she could see rays of light shooting from the object which had again appeared to keep station with her car until she arrived home. At one time during the journey the object travelled near her and the rays seemed to come towards the right-hand side of her car.

She felt a bump against that side as if they had struck it. At this moment she felt as if she had received an electric shock and had felt a severe pain in her neck. The left-hand side headlight of the car also went out. This made her extremely frightened. When she got home she felt very ill and had complained to her parents. This object had emitted brilliant lights and radiation beams. On arriving home her daughter had been in a distressed condition and she had discovered marks on the car, which she considered were burn marks.

The object again remained stationary in the sky north of her home and had not been seen by her parents. They had noticed it for a short time before going inside her home. There had been no sign of the object on the following morning. Miss Foulkes' parents confirmed seeing an object in the sky on both occasions as described by their daughter and agreed with her descriptions of these.

A Second Source Surfaces

When Diane asked Corporal Rickwood for his opinion on the strange affair, he was decidedly noncommittal, stating only that, and I quote again from the file, "the incident was in no way connected with the Royal Air Force or the Armed Forces." Diane replied that she had reached that conclusion herself, too, but it still didn't help her to understand what it was that she encountered—not just once, but twice over the course of a couple of years. It was at this point in the discussion that Diane revealed yet another eye-opening aspect of the story.

In the P&SS documentation, it reads as follows: "Miss Foulkes further stated that she believed that the objects could be associated with a Mr. Griffin who lived in the area and who is reputed to have made contact with these objects and actually entered one and met one of the occupants. He is also alleged to make his contacts with them at Montford Bridge."

After a few more minutes of going over the story, it was time for the P&SS team to leave. They thanked Diane and her parents for taking the time to speak with them—and for the tea too—and headed off into the night. Several days later, Diane received a letter addressed to her and which came from RAF Shawbury. The letter revealed that Diane's case had been carefully examined, but remained unexplainable. She never heard from them again. But someone heard from them: Mr. Griffin.

A Tale of Abduction Comes Tumbling Out

That Griffin isn't an overly common name—and particularly so among the small and picturesque villages of Shropshire—meant it didn't take the Provost and Security Services very long at all to find the man Foulkes had mentioned in her story to the P&SS. In fact, they were knocking on Griffin's door only two days after speaking to her. Curiously, in the now-declassified papers on Mr. Griffin, his first name is deleted, as is his address at the time. But the story is there for all to see. According to Mr. Griffin, and just like Diane, he had had several encounters at Montford Bridge, which is also the name of the village in which the centuries-old bridge still stands.

All of Mr. Griffin's encounters occurred in the early hours of the morning, and always after he was overcome by an uncanny compulsion to drive out to the bridge, park his car as close to the bridge as he could—without causing a potential accident—and then wait. And wait. He told the P&SS unit—once again under Corporal Rickwood—that finally he would see a large, blue light in the sky. In moments, his mind would become hazy and he would find himself laid out on a large and long "table," which was surrounded by what he described as a group of "pixies." In other words, small humanoid figures. The Greys? In all likelihood, yes.

When questioned about what happened next, Mr. Griffin said that on every occasion he felt he was helping the creatures with "their experiments," but what those experiments were, exactly, he could not remember. Just like Betty and Barney Hill, Mr. Griffin's memory was not as it should have been. The aliens had clearly hit the "delete button" on the most important aspects of Mr. Griffin's abductions.

Mr. Griffin apologized for the fact that certain portions of the story were missing from his mind, but this did not seem to disappoint Corporal Rickwood's team. In fact, before leaving they asked if he would be willing to be interviewed by a psychologist from the Ministry of Defense, which is equivalent to the United States Department of Defense (DoD). The files do not reflect if Mr. Griffin was interviewed by MoD specialists. But just the fact that such a suggestion was made implies that the P&SS may have had earlier successes in this area of medicine when it came to trying to uncover the missing memories of someone taken onboard an extraterrestrial spaceship.

For the Ministry of Defense, this was further evidence that the alien abduction phenomenon was very much a growing one—something which left them decidedly uneasy.

9 "UNDERSIZED CREATURES SIMILAR TO MEMBERS OF THE HUMAN RACE"

Although the FBI has declassified thousands of pages on the contactee movement of the 1950s and later, they have released just one document pertaining to the alien abduction issue. It dates from 1967 and describes—albeit briefly—what sounds like a classic abduction experience. Notably, the FBI shared the data and the document with an agency whose name has been deliberately blacked out in the relevant papers.

The specific date is January 18, 1967, and is captioned as follows: "Unidentified Flying Object Allegedly Sighting [sic], January 17, 1967." It reads thus:

At 4:10 a.m., January 18, 1967, [deleted] advised that he desired to report that he had observed a large oblong-shaped object which alighted in the street in front of him when he was on his way home from his television repair shop, the [deleted], Chesapeake, Virginia. He believes that he was taken into this craft which he recalls as being made of a glass-like substance and being transparent. It was manned by several individuals who appeared to be undersized creatures similar to members of the human race, probably not more than 4 feet tall. They were allegedly wearing regular trouser pants and T-shirts. [deleted] believes that he was transported by this craft for an undetermined distance and returned to his point of take-off approximately one hour later.

[Deleted] spoke in a coherent manner although he appeared to be under certain emotional strain. He claimed he had not been drinking any intoxicants but he was unable to account for the time between 8:00 p.m. and 4:00 a.m. He stated he was telephoning from his workshop but had no recollection of being elsewhere between 8:00 p.m. and 4:00 a.m.

While the reference to the aliens allegedly wearing "regular" clothing is admittedly strange, there is no denying the fact that the experience closely mirrors those of so many others. There was, for example, the fact that the aliens were "not more than 4 feet tall," which strongly suggests the man's captors were of the Grey alien kind. And that the victim "was unable to account for the time between 8:00 p.m. and 4:00 a.m." is prime evidence of the phenomenon of missing time.

It's also worth noting that that description of the craft's transparency matches another account made eight years later. In 1975, when he was abducted from the heart of Arizona's Sitgreaves National Forest, logger Travis Walton described how at one point the walls of the craft onto which he was taken were temporarily made transparent—to the extent that he could see the stars surrounding the UFO as it soared across the skies. This transparency of the craft sounds not unlike the description in the FBI report. Recall that the FBI stated the witness "believes that he was taken into this craft which he recalls as being made of a glass-like substance and being transparent."

What this tells us is that even though the report is brief in nature and content, it demonstrates that in all probability the witness had a genuine alien abduction experience—one which became the subject of an FBI report and which was shared with another, unknown, agency. There is one other issue, too, that needs highlighting. In fact, it's the most significant part of the story.

A New Lead in the Story

I briefly mentioned this case—and the attendant documentation—in an article for the Australian website Mysterious Universe in September 2015, called "Government Files on Alien Abductees?" As so often happens when I write online articles, people contact me to share their stories. One of those who wanted to provide input on this particular affair was none other than the granddaughter of the TV repairman. For reasons that will soon become apparent, I have given the source an alias, "Jennifer."

Jennifer first contacted me about ten months after the article was published. As she explained, she was of two minds about whether or not to share what she knew, out of fear that there might be some kind of retaliation. I asked from whom. Jennifer replied: "The government." This was, to say the least, intriguing.

Jennifer said that within her close-knit family, the events of that January 1967 encounter were well known, even though they kept the tale pretty much to themselves. In the wake of what went down, her grandfather and grandmother had developed a deep interest in the UFO phenomenon and built up a large library of books on the topic. Jennifer too had developed a fascination for UFOs, particularly the abduction phenomenon. This is hardly surprising, given her grandfather's encounter. When she read my article, Jennifer was utterly amazed to see that the FBI's record on the encounter was now in the public domain. In fact, the document was declassified in 1977, but it had not had any real, meaningful publicity until I mentioned it in the *Mysterious Universe* article.

Sharing a Sensational Story

I asked for some proof that Jennifer was indeed who she claimed to be—namely, the granddaughter of the man in question. As luck would have it, Jennifer was living in San Diego, and I was due to speak for several West Coast UFO groups, including the Orange County, California–based chapter of the Mutual UFO Network (MUFON), in about a month. So it was the perfect time to meet, which is precisely what we did.

Jennifer drove up from San Diego, and she had the foresight to bring evidence of who she was—and of who her grandfather was, too, including a few old black-and-white photos of him smiling proudly outside of his Chesapeake TV repair shop. She *was* who she claimed to be; that was a very good sign. Then we got down to business. Over drinks in my Orange County hotel, the whole story came out. To say the experience was revealing would be an understatement.

Jennifer said that the only response from the FBI was a single phone call to her grandfather informing him that they would be forwarding the report to another agency—in the event that they might be interested in the story. It was a cordial conversation that lasted just a few minutes. Four days later, there was a knock at the door. It was a pair of men in military uniforms. They identified themselves as working for US Air Force intelligence, which was confirmed by their ID cards.

Although Jennifer's grandfather was a bit perturbed to see a pair of military personnel on his doorstep, he invited them in. There followed an in-depth question-and-answer session which lasted for more than an hour.

Abductions, Aliens, and an Apocalyptic Nightmare

It was clear, Jennifer said, that the two men had deep knowledge of the alien abduction phenomenon. They wanted to know more about the missing time which had been reported. They were particularly interested in—and concerned about—the no less than eight hours that could not be accounted for. The pair wanted to know if, in the period between reporting to the FBI what had happened and the time of their visit, Jennifer's grandfather had any unusual dreams: nightmares of being taken onboard a UFO and subjected to strange medical experiments. While some might consider this to be a case of leading the witness, Jennifer's grandfather said that, yes, he actually had had two odd dreams—one of him "floating" out of bed, as Jennifer worded it, and being taken to a small, round room which was brightly lit and filled with an odor of burning metal. He had vague memories of seeing three small creatures ushering him to what looked like a gurney. Then, nothing. As for the other dream, it was of a nuclear explosion—a massive detonation which left Washington, DC, in ruins and millions dead and dying. The issue of apocalyptic dreams in relation to the alien abduction phenomenon is something we'll come back to in a later chapter.

Jennifer's grandfather was asked if he would be willing to undergo a thorough medical examination at a military hospital, which he declined. The two men did not push the issue when he replied in the negative. The pair then turned their attentions to the "glass"-like nature of the UFO. This, said Jennifer, was an area that the men seemed particularly interested in. Her grandfather came straight to the point: the UFO was solid but had the ability to become transparent, which sounds just like what abductee Travis Walton would later describe in 1975. The glass-like reference, the military men were told, was to how the walls would briefly change from being solid and white in color to completely see-through.

There were a couple other curious questions, too:

1. Had anyone else in the family experienced anything similar?

2. Did the witness feel threatened by the encounter?

The answers were "no" to the first question and "yes" to the second. With that, the men stood up, thanked Jennifer's grandfather for his time and cooperation, and requested that he not talk of their visit. Their parting words were to the effect of "If we have any more questions, can we speak to you again?" Jennifer's grandfather said he would be pleased to speak with them at any time. No follow-up visit ever came, however. At least, not a normal visit. The most sinister saga of the story was still to come.

A Warning from a Man in Black

Roughly four or five days after the two men from Air Force intelligence came calling, Jennifer's grandfather found himself being watched by someone else. Nothing less than a definitive Man in Black. Whenever the likes of the MIB are brought up, it inevitably provokes imagery of Will Smith and Tommy Lee Jones. This is hardly surprising, as the three *Men in Black* movies were phenomenally successful.

It's important to note, however, that the *real* MIB are nothing like their movie counterparts. In the films, the MIB work for a government agency that answers to no one. The genuine MIB—on which the movie versions were based—are very different. They are pale-skinned, cadaverous creatures with large, hypnotic eyes who typically wear old-style fedora hats and black suits. They have the ability to control people's minds, to hypnotize them, and even to cause physical sickness and illness—as if the witnesses to the MIB have somehow been supernaturally infected. In other words, the MIB of the real world are far more like Gothic vampires than government agents. This has given rise to the possibility that the MIB may well be human–alien hybrids, of a type similar to those described in David Jacobs's 2015 book, *Walking Among Us*. All of this brings us back to Jennifer.

Jennifer told me that on three occasions, her grandfather was followed along the Chesapeake streets by a very tall and thin man dressed in a black suit and a black trench coat. This would have been in early February 1967, a few weeks after the encounter which caught the attention of both the FBI and the Air Force. On one occasion, the MIB shadowed Jennifer's grandfather to his local pool joint, where he hung out with his buddies on Friday night. On another occasion, the Man in Black suddenly appeared in the TV repair shop which Jennifer's grandfather owned. The MIB approached the counter, offering nothing but a terrifying, insane grin, turned around, and left the store. Jennifer said her grandfather was too shocked and traumatized to do anything but stand there, frozen to the spot. The third and final time the MIB appeared was equally disturbing. As a keen fisherman, Jennifer's grandfather often spent time on the banks of a nearby river. Three days after the encounter in the store, the MIB suddenly appeared—as if out of nowhere—on the other side of the river, staring malevolently. And then, suddenly, he vanished—as in *literally* vanished. Gone. Dematerialized.

That was more than enough and was the primary reason why the family had chosen not to say anything—at least, not until I highlighted the FBI document in my 2015 article. It just goes to show how some of the most amazing stories surface under such unlikely circumstances. And, of course, it raises another question: How many other abductees—just like Jennifer's grandfather—have chosen not to share the details of their traumatic abduction encounters, after being silenced by the mysterious Men in Black?

10 THE RISE OF THE BLACK HELICOPTERS

I n the early to mid-1970s, a new component was added to the ongoing alien abduction phenomenon. It all revolved around what has become notoriously known in the field of ufology as the "black helicopter." Since at least 1973, there have been numerous reports of helicopters—black in color and with no visible markings or identifying numbers—flying around, usually after dark, and in the vicinity of the homes of those who have been subjected to alien abductions. The most prevalent theory within the domain of UFO research is that the black helicopters are attached to quick-reaction military teams, whose job it is to respond to UFO—and abduction-based—incidents in a rapid fashion. Before we get to the matter of the connection between the black helicopters and alien abductions, let's first take a look at how the phenomenon began.

The 1970s saw the increase of two phenomena in the United States: alien abductions and cattle mutilations. We have seen that alien abductions date back to the 1950s. As for cattle mutilations, they largely began in the mid-1960s. It's surely no coincidence at all, though, that when both mysteries increased to incredible degrees in the 1970s, the presence of the black helicopters became almost overwhelming. Abductees told of seeing large, double-rotor helicopters over their homes late at night. Ranchers complained to their local authorities that black 'copters were flying low over their fields—also late at night and in the very same areas where their cattle were found dead, with organs removed from their bodies, blood drained to a huge degree, and evidence of what looked like laser technology utilized to open up the bodies of the poor animals.

The subject gets even more confusing and controversial: in some cases the witnesses described the black helicopters flying in complete silence. Others swore that the helicopters vanished in a flash of light—something which has led some UFO researchers to conclude that the helicopters are really alien spacecraft which have the ability to change their appearance into multiple forms, including that of a helicopter, as we'll see soon.

The British Police Force Secretly Gets Involved

There is no doubt that the rise of the black helicopter phenomenon began in the early to mid-1970s—and they weren't just seen in the United States. Let's take a look at a few such cases. In 1973, a number of profound alien abduction incidents were reported in the United Kingdom. And sightings of black helicopters were not just rife: nothing less than an epidemic of reports was going down at the very same time. The familiar beating sounds of helicopters were heard above the homes of abductees. Intimidating men dressed in black, who knew all about the private lives of the abductees under surveillance, issued warnings not to talk about what they had seen and experienced.

Although those helicopter-based incidents began to be reported in the United Kingdom around September 1973, it wasn't until shortly after the new year that word got out regarding what was afoot. It was thanks to the media that the story reached the public. An insider source in the British government quietly informed the press that an arm of the British police force—Special Branch—was secretly investigating reports of unidentified helicopters all across the United Kingdom. Initial fears were that the helicopters were flown by terrorists who were getting ready to launch attacks across the country; maybe the Irish Republican Army, a collective bunch of scum who did engage in cowardly attacks on the United Kingdom in the 1970s and onward. No wonder, then, that Special Branch quickly got involved. It soon turned out, though, that there was no data at all to support the idea that terrorists were the culprits. So who was responsible? When the story hit the nation's media, Special Branch released a statement which confirmed their officers were deeply involved in an investigation of the mysterious helicopters, but admittedly had very few answers.

One of the areas hit by the helicopter invasions was the English county of Cheshire. In response to this onslaught of sightings, the Cheshire police force released the following statement:

We don't know of any reason why the helicopter should make these trips at night. Obviously we are anxious to find out. Apart from anything else, the helicopter crosses one of the main flight paths to Manchester Airport. There is an obvious danger to the aircraft going into the airport. We are very interested to know what is happening. We hope to be able to trace the pilot and put some suggestions to him. It would appear the pilot is in breach of civil aviation laws. A special license is needed to fly a helicopter at night.

Within days, the Derbyshire police force circulated its own statement to the press and the BBC: "All sorts of things spring to mind but we have pretty much ruled out that it is anything to do with illegal immigrants, and nothing appears to have been stolen in the areas where the aircraft has been sighted."

Files Are Finally Released

At the time, not much more was known about the strange helicopters. Today, however, it's a very different situation. In the 2000s, and as a result of the provisions of the UK Freedom of Information Act, Special Branch

MEMORANDUM

CHIEF SUPT. 'B' SQUAD

1.   At 2 pm today, 21 March 1974, a meeting was held at
Horseferry House with D H J Hilary in the Chair to discuss
a number of unexplained helicopter sightings at night,
mainly reported to the police in Derbyshire.

2.   Present were Messrs Clayton, McQueen and Montgomery-Pott
of Home Office, Assistant Chief Constable Bowers (Derby
County and Borough Constabulary), Assistant Chief Constable
Laugharne and Superintendent Dean (Cheshire Constabulary),
and two Ministry of Defence representatives. ████████████
████████████████

3.   The meeting discussed the authenticity of the numerous
sightings reported during the end of 1973 and January 1974,
together with some allegedly corroborative reports available
through the Civil Aviation Authority, from the Air Traffic
Control Centre at Preston and Manchester Air Traffic Control.

4.   In the event there were found to be only three 'hard'
sightings and no useful pattern of timing or positioning
was discernible; in addition, no crimes were reported at the
times of the alleged flights. I was able to report that the
Metropolitan Police Special Branch had no hard information
to place potential subversive activities in the area.

5.   However, it was agreed that the sightings could not be
ignored and MOD were asked what facilities they could provide
to assist with identifying the helicopter. The use of
searchlights, radar, MOD helicopters, and the Harrier Jump Jet
were discussed but considered either impractical or too
expensive.

The UK government addresses the "Phantom Helicopter" phenomenon (courtesy
of the UK government)

finally released its dossier on the mysterious helicopters. One of the most intriguing files in the large collection of material is titled "Alleged Unauthorized Helicopter Flights in Derbyshire and Cheshire."

A Special Branch officer whose name is deleted from the now-declassified files writes:

The machine was observed on a number of occasions over a period of two weeks to be apparently practicing landings in the vicinity of the sites of quarries and explosive stores in the Derbyshire countryside. Special Branch Constable [deleted] has made numerous enquiries to discover the ownership and reasons for the flights from various sources but has yet to establish any positive facts. He has contacted an experienced Royal Air Force helicopter pilot with night flying experience who explained that night flying in the Derbyshire areas would be extremely dangerous due to the nature of the terrain and to the number of overhead pylons in the area.

Roughly eight weeks after Special Branch began to dig further into the Derbyshire-based encounters, a clandestine meeting was held in the heart of London, which was attended by representatives of Special Branch, MI5—which is the UK equivalent of the FBI—and the Ministry of Defense. Further into 1974, ambitious plans were made to have military fighter planes pursue the helicopters and force their pilots to land their craft. Rather notably, in the immediate aftermath of this decision, the wave of helicopter encounters in the United Kingdom came to a sudden end.

The Alien Abduction Connection

Ufologists have speculated—and probably correctly—that the helicopters were attached to a highly secret program of the British government designed to monitor the abductees. And when Special Branch began poking their nose in, they were quietly told by the military to back off; that this was an issue concerning national security, one which could not risk being compromised. The result: Special Branch did indeed back off, and the investigations into the helicopter waves of 1973–1974 were suddenly over.

One final thing on the UK wave: also in 1974, one of the most bizarre and profound alien abduction experiences occurred. The location was the village of Aveley, which is located in the English county of Essex. As the Avis family was driving home late at night, they suddenly encountered an egg-shaped, blue light shadowing their car. Then, to their fear, a green fog covered the car. There was an overwhelming silence—not even the car's engine could be heard. Then, suddenly, it was all over. Or so it seemed. Bad dreams—of alien encounters and of being taken onboard an extraterrestrial craft—dominated their sleep. Imagery of being experimented on by dwarfish creatures soon followed. Investigations undertaken by UFO researchers Andrew Collins and Barry King uncovered nothing less than a full-blown abduction experience.

Intriguingly, the Avis family experienced problems with their telephone: strange clicks could be heard whenever they picked the phone up—as if their line was tapped, perhaps by someone in the military or the intelligence community who had opened a file on them. Given that there was a widespread wave of black helicopters around the same time, a strong case can be made that someone was going to extraordinary lengths to keep the UK abductees under careful watch.

Now, let's see what was going on in the United States of an almost identical nature and in the same time frame.

Cattle Mutilations and Alien Abductions

At this stage in the story, it's important to note the links among the black helicopters, alien abductions, and what have infamously become known as cattle mutilations. The reason will soon become graphically apparent.

Judy Doraty was someone who, on the night of May 23, 1973, most definitely found herself in the wrong place at the wrong time. As a result, she became the subject of a highly classified US Air Force intelligence file.

On the star-filled night when her world was ripped apart, Doraty was driving home from a bingo game outside Houston. Also along for the game and the drive home were Doraty's teenage daughter, her brother-in-law, her sister, and her mother. They had a great time. But something was about to intervene in a terrifying way.

As the drive progressed, the family caught sight of a strange, large bright light in the sky. They were all perplexed—and even a bit concerned—by the fact that the object seemed to be shadowing them: wherever they drove, the light seemed to follow. At first, they thought it might have been a helicopter heading for Galveston's airport, Scholes International Airport. But a careful look revealed it was not a helicopter, after all. It was . . . *something else*. This was not a good sign. It only proceeded to get worse.

As Judy reached a darkened pasture in a rural area, she brought the car to a stop and got out. The light in the sky—seemingly responding to her actions—suddenly came closer. *Much* closer. In seconds, and to their complete amazement and shock, the light could now be seen for what it really was: a massive, circular craft which swooped silently and effortlessly over them. It then headed toward a nearby field and, as the group looked on, shot vertically into the sky and vanished in seconds. Or that's what *seemed* to have happened. Like so many people who have been subjected to the alien abduction experience, in the days that followed what was clearly a *very* close encounter, Judy began to realize that there had been more to the encounter than she consciously realized. Her dreams became outright nightmares. They were filled with terror and graphic images of UFOs. Fragments of disturbing memories were fighting to be freed from Judy's subconscious. For years, though, Judy suffered in silence with pummeling headaches and those awful dreams.

Seven Years Later, an Almost Identical Encounter

It wasn't until 1980—when Judy Doraty was hypnotized by Professor Leo Sprinkle of the University of Wyoming—that the full picture became clear.

Just like Betty and Barney Hill more than a decade earlier, Doraty's mind had been wiped to a huge degree. At least, until Sprinkle was able to retrieve some of that missing time. In her hypnotized state, Doraty recalled getting out of the car and then seeing a spotlight hit the trunk. This was no normal spotlight, however. Doraty said that the light seemed to have what she called "substance" to it. Somehow, the light lifted a struggling, squirming brown-and-white calf into the air from the same field near where the family had stopped. Then, something very weird happened.

Although, under hypnosis, Doraty recalled being outside of her vehicle, and on the ground, it was as if her mind had somehow been relocated to the craft. She seemed to have recall of two very different things, but which were going on simultaneously. She told a horrific story: the calf was rapidly and systematically dissected and its body was dropped backed to the ground with a thud. Doraty also had vague memories under hypnosis of her daughter having been abducted and examined, but by whom and why remained unclear. It was a trauma-filled experience which may have given Doraty a significant number of answers, but which hardly made her feel relaxed.

Under hypnosis, and in terms of the violent mutilation and killing of the calf, Doraty said the aliens, "[have] been testing, they've been here for quite some time and they test the soil as well as our water, as well as our animal life and vegetation. There's a lot involved. More than just pollution. Their concern is loss of life. There is going to be a big loss of life due to this." When questioned further, Judy answered that the loss of life would be due to "nuclear waste or testing."

Under circumstances which remain murky to this very day, although Judy Doraty was not interviewed until 1980, someone else knew about her encounter—and of the cattle mutilation, too—almost immediately. A seventeen-page document on Doraty's experience was created in June 1973, just one month after the incident occurred. By whom? Air Force intelligence at Kirtland Air Force Base, New Mexico. We know this because one of the people involved in the preparation, who called himself "Stigliano," revealed his knowledge of the situation. He claimed that unbeknown to Doraty, this was not her first abduction experience. It was, he maintained, her *third*.

Stigliano further claimed that Doraty had been watched for a number of months, something which led to the compilation of a file on her. The military unit that was concerned about Doraty's abduction experiences was also looking into links to the growing cattle mutilation, believing there was a direct connection, although in what way they weren't fully sure. And now, with the Doraty case, they had made a direct connection between the two phenomena. In that sense, asserted Stigliano, the Doraty affair was one of the most important of all: the shadowy investigation—and the creation of the file—had revealed a largely unknown and sinister agenda at work. Somehow, the Air Force suspected, alien abductions and cattle mutilations were interconnected.

For those who may think this sounds like the kind of thing one might see on an episode of *The X-Files*, it's not. Now, it's time to take a look at a large batch of official FBI files on cattle mutilations. Those same FBI files just happen to be filled with tales of black helicopters.

11 ABDUCTED: BUT BY ALIENS OR THE MILITARY?

The month of October 1973 was one that will go down in UFO history. It was a month in which the United States was swamped by intrusions from UFOs. The late Leonard Stringfield—a UFO researcher and former intelligence officer with the US Air Force— was someone who lived through that astonishing flying saucer wave and who offered the following recollections:

The tornadic effect of 1973's flap was to stun a nation already troubled by Watergate and a Middle East crisis. At its peak, October 17—in one 24-hour period—there were more than fifty cities and towns reporting concentrated UFO activity. Switchboards of the news media and police were jammed by calls from frightened citizens. Many reported extraordinary lighted objects at low levels; others claimed closer encounters.

Of those closer encounters, one really stands out. It's an encounter which gets to the very crux of this book. It involved two men who, before they were abducted by strange beings on a Mississippi river, were doing nothing stranger than a spot of fishing.

Taken

The night of October 10, 1973, was one that Calvin Parker and Charles Hickson would not forget. And it all began in a perfectly normal, relaxed fashion. Forty-two-year-old Hickson and nineteen-year-old Parker worked together and often spent time fishing on the Pascagoula River in southeastern Mississippi. It was about nine on a dark and fateful night when their world came tumbling down around them. For a while the fish were biting. It would, however, not be long before the two men would find themselves reeled in—though "hauled in" might be a better way of putting it.

As they sat on the banks of the river, the two could see there was an odd, blue, flickering light in the distance—odd in the sense that it seemed to be following the contours of the river, but slightly above it. Both Hickson and Parker stared at it, trying to figure out what on earth it was. Earth may very well have had nothing to do with it. Helicopter? they wondered. But there was no noise. An aircraft? It was way too low and slow. Someone's idea of a joke? If only.

When the strange whatever-it-was got closer, a stark realization quickly hit both men: this was like nothing they had ever seen before. It was a fairly small craft, oval in design, and illuminated—almost glowing. And a vomit-inducing, deep droning sound suddenly enveloped them. Things seemed strange, unreal, dreamlike, as the pair tried to scramble away. No such luck: in seconds both Parker and Hickson were rendered almost unable to move. Suddenly, the craft came very close—perilously so—and a doorway opened. The two men stared in confused horror as three entities of a bizarre appearance levitated through the doorway and, for a few seconds, were suspended in the air—staring directly at the two freaked-out fishermen. Things went from bad to worse: the creatures, which were basically humanoid, had strange faces that resembled tight-fitting masks, with three pen-like protrusions sticking out of their heads. Their hands were crab-like. (Hickson would later correct this by referring to them as "lobster"-like.) The creatures maneuvered in the direction of the men. In his disoriented state, Hickson could only stare at the things as they got closer and closer.

Parker, however, hyperventilating to an extreme degree, keeled over in a dead faint.

Parker started to come around but found himself unable to move. Hickson too was hit by sudden paralysis. The aliens lunged forward, grabbed both men, and steered the pair to the craft. They were taken onboard and subjected to the usual fear-inducing experiments of the kind the Greys are notoriously known for. In this case, the pair was placed onto table-like structures, and a device that was described as a "big eye" hovered over the immobile men, seemingly scrutinizing them from head to toe. When the procedure was over, they were dropped back on the bank. Now they knew how the average fish felt on a Saturday night.

It didn't take long for the pair to gather their wits—it was as if whatever had rendered them immobile was not long-lasting. Finally, the two were able to scramble up the bank, get in their vehicle, and race to the sheriff's office. The story surfaced in rollercoaster style. The media was soon on the trail of the pair. But so was the military—and they got there first.

Two Men and the Military

In no time at all after contacting the police, Parker and Hickson were whisked off to Keesler Air Force Base in Biloxi, on the Mississippi Gulf Coast. They were driven there by a local police officer, Deputy Tom Huntley, who later made an intriguing statement: "We were in an unmarked car but the guards were expecting us and waved us through the moment I said who I was. I looked back through my rear-view mirror, and damn if two cars full of air police hadn't fallen in behind us. They had more air police stationed at each crossing all along the road."

Officer Huntley eventually revealed much more, too: on being directed to one particular building, a team of medical personnel were already there, awaiting the arrival of Hickson and Parker. Huntley said that after he and Parker and Hickson were directed into the building, a series of tests quickly began. Of the doctors, Huntley added that they "looked like space creatures—all wrapped in white and masked and gloved." Both men had a Geiger counter run over them. Their fingers and shoes were swabbed—with each swab carefully placed into a separate bottle.

John Keel, of *The Mothman Prophecies* fame, said something notable when the story of the military's involvement got out: "It was clear the Air Force doctors knew what they were doing and had probably done it many times before. After the examination was completed, Huntley, Hickson, and Parker were escorted to another building."

Of this other facility, Officer Huntley stated, "It was something. Armed air police at each door and all along the route. Four of them in the conference room. And the brass—colonels, majors—the whole base command must have been there. And a heap of doctors."

Back to Keel: "The intriguing part of this is the extensive security measures taken. It sounds as if the whole base had been put on alert for the occasion, and the two contactees were so closely guarded during their visit that it seems as if the Air Force expected them to blow up the base. To me, this Keesler Air Force Base investigation was far more interesting than the UFO contact itself."

In light of all the above, one has to wonder just how many secret dossiers on Parker and Hickson were created by the Air Force on that strange and mysterious day. We do know that Hickson found himself a victim of endless odd phone calls, which went on for months, suggesting someone was keeping an eye on him.

As for the two men, their lives went in very different directions. Parker all but completely shunned the limelight, having suffered a nervous collapse after the incident, and he continues to largely avoid speaking about the events of October 10, 1973. Hickson, however, embraced it all, and with writer William Mendez wrote a book on the case titled *UFO Contact at Pascagoula*. Hickson passed away in September 2011.

A Repeat of the Antonio Villas Boas Case?

There is another aspect to this very curious affair which must be addressed. It's the possibility that the entire event was not an alien abduction, but a

MILAB-driven event. Sounds impossible? It may not be: only a very short distance from where Parker and Hickson were kidnapped is a small area called Horn Island. It looks pleasant and inviting, which it is. But that wasn't always the case. When the Second World War was still raging, Horn Island was home to top-secret research in the fields of chemical and biological warfare. Less than a decade later, the US Army's Chemical Corps used the island for its early research into hypnosis, mind control, and psychedelics—in essence, to see how the human mind could be altered, and radically so, too.

The history books state that all such work on Horn Island was halted in the 1960s—amid rumors that some of the locals ended up in altered states after being accidentally hit by powerful aerosol-based hallucinogenic substances carried by the wind. But try asking the locals about when things really ended and you'll get a very different response. There are tales of the Army secretly employing the use of BZ in the area in the early 1970s. And what might BZ be? Known as "Buzz," it's a powerful mind-mixer, the official title of which is 3-quinuclidinyl benzilate. Graphic hallucinations are typical, as are states of unreality. Cognitive dysfunction soon sets in. Then, incapacitation.

Perhaps, while in a BZ-driven state, Parker and Hickson did not encounter a UFO, but rather one of those black helicopters that play such a deep role in the monitoring of alien abductees. Maybe the masklike faces of the "aliens" were exactly that: masks. Perhaps the crab-like hands that the men said they saw were actually thick gloves, attached to equally thick protective suits, designed to prevent the all-too-human people inside those suits from being affected. When you look at all the data, such a scenario does not sound at all unlikely. This does, however, leave us with an important question.

Why would the Air Force even want to go to such lengths? Consider this as a possibility: the October 1973 UFO wave was at its height. The military was clearly concerned by this sudden invasion of US airspace. But let's go with that scenario discussed in a previous chapter—namely, that the government might stage such incidents to have the aliens appear to us as dangerous and evil, when they may actually be benign and friendly. It must be said that the Pascagoula incident was filled with nothing but negativity and terror. Calvin Parker passed out, suffered a nervous breakdown, and retreated into the shadows. Both men were confronted by creatures which looked extremely sinister and which manhandled the pair in a rough and terrifying fashion.

If the UFO wave of 1973 was indeed one of benign proportions— but the government wanted to give the aliens a very bad rap—all things suddenly make sense. Even the location, which had been a hotbed for top secret, government-controlled, mind-altering programs for decades.

12 CATTLE MUTILATIONS, BLACK HELICOPTERS, AND THE FBI

t's most intriguing to note that in the United States the black helicopter phenomenon began in 1973—the very same year in which the United Kingdom was *also* hit by a wave of helicopter-based incidents, and which prompted the British police force's Special Branch to launch an investigation. In the United States, things started in the Hawkeye State: Iowa. For the first three months of the year, outraged farmers contacted local law enforcement with strange and unsettling stories: they would wake up in the morning, head to their fields, and find several of their cattle dead. These were no normal deaths, though. The cows' genitals were gone, as were their eyeballs. Their skin appeared to have been opened with some kind of device employing incredible temperatures, maybe a laser-based device. Organs were not savagely torn out, as they might have been if coyotes were the culprits. Instead, they were carefully cut out. Under cover of darkness, an unstoppable force was causing mayhem throughout rural Iowa.

It wasn't long before those same ranchers had something else to deal with. You have probably already guessed what that was. That's right: black helicopters. But were the pilots of the craft performing the mutilations? Or were they monitoring the activities of the mutilators, who may not even have been human? These were the questions being asked seriously—and particularly so after sunset, when farmers wondered and dreaded what they might find when a new day dawned. Even local law enforcement was open to the idea that something from another realm of existence just might have been behind the mutilation wave.

When the Iowa cases were at their height, local police called in the FBI. Despite the large amount of testimony, photographs, necropsy reports, and extensive police files, the FBI stayed curiously out of the controversy. They maintained that since the events didn't amount to "interstate transportation of the maimed animals," they were powerless to get involved. The FBI, then, didn't deny the reality of the grisly killings, but kept their distance because of bureaucratic reasons.

When, in the fall of 1974, Nebraska was next on the hit list, Senator Carl T. Curtis, who served in the US Senate from 1955 to 1979, wanted answers—and he wanted those answers quickly. Such was Curtis's level of concern that he went right to the director of the FBI, Clarence M. Kelley, who had just a year prior had taken on the position after the death of J. Edgar Hoover. Once again, though, the FBI took the stance that this was an area outside their jurisdiction. Rumors abounded that the FBI had been warned to keep away from the subject. But who would have the power and influence to ensure the FBI would stay away? It was a notable question.

The Mutes Become an Epidemic

By 1975, things had gotten to the point where the FBI could no longer ignore what was going on. Exasperated by a wave of mutes in his state of Colorado in 1975, Senator Floyd K. Haskell sent the following letter to FBI Director Kelley:

For several months my office has been receiving reports of cattle mutilations throughout Colorado and other western states. At least 130 cases in Colorado alone have been reported to local officials and the

Colorado Bureau of Investigation (CBI); the CBI has verified that the incidents have occurred for the last two years in nine states. The ranchers and rural residents of Colorado are concerned and frightened by these incidents. The bizarre mutilations are frightening in themselves: in virtually all the cases, the left ear, rectum and sex organ of each animal has been cut away and the blood drained from the carcass, but with no traces of blood left on the ground and no footprints.

If 130-plus incidents were not nearly enough to get the FBI involved, there was the matter of the black helicopters, which had also caught the attention of Senator Haskell. He added, "*In Colorado's Morgan County area there has also been reports that a helicopter was used by those who mutilated the carcasses of the cattle, and several persons have reported being chased by a similar helicopter* [italics mine]. Because I am gravely concerned by this situation, I am asking that the Federal Bureau of Investigation enter the case."

The senator signed off: "Although the CBI has been investigating the incidents, and local officials also have been involved, the lack of a central unified direction has frustrated the investigation. It seems to have progressed little, except for the recognition at long last that the incidents must be taken seriously. Now it appears that ranchers are arming themselves to protect their livestock, as well as their families and themselves, because they are frustrated by the unsuccessful investigation. Clearly something must be done before someone gets hurt."

I mentioned above that the FBI could not ignore the Colorado attacks and the attendant helicopter-based incidents. That's true: the FBI carefully collected numerous reports from state senators and police departments. But that's all they did: they filed the reports away and chose not to look into the matter at all. This, again, led to theories that someone had ordered the FBI to back off. Finally, though, the time came when the FBI realized that it could not continue to stonewall those affected by these incidents and had to do something. For the ranchers, *anything* was better than *nothing*.

The year 1978 was pivotal: Senator Harrison Schmitt of New Mexico—an astronaut who walked on the moon in 1972—expressed his deep concerns to the FBI about the mutilations, angry farmers, and those unidentified helicopters. Senator Schmitt was driven to contact the FBI as a result of a tremendous amount of work in this area which had been undertaken by a police officer from Rio Arriba County, New Mexico. His name was Gabe Valdez. It turns out that Valdez had been carefully collating reports—and coming to his own extraordinary conclusions—since 1975. This almost unique collection of data was copied to the FBI in 1978, which finally realized that they had to be seen at least doing something. As 1978 became 1979, the FBI's assistant attorney took steps to have all the relevant Valdez papers made available to various offices within the FBI. To a degree, an investigation began.

One only has to take a look at Officer Valdez's carefully and scrupulously prepared papers to see that something extremely sinister was at work. Consider the following, from the summer of 1976.

Radiation, Mysterious "Tripods," and Dead Cattle

Valdez recorded the facts of a deeply unsettling case he had personally looked into:

Investigations around the area revealed that a suspected aircraft of some type had landed twice, leaving three pod marks positioned in a triangular shape. The diameter of each pod was 14 inches. Emanating from the two landings were smaller triangular shaped tripods 28 inches and 4 inches in diameter. Investigation at the scene showed that these small tripods had followed the cow for approximately 600 feet. Tracks of the cow showed where she had struggled and fallen. The small tripod tracks were all around the cow. Other evidence showed that grass around the tripods, as they followed the cow, had been scorched. Also a yellow oily substance was located in two places under the small tripods. This substance was submitted to the State Police Lab. The Lab was unable to detect the content of the substance.

A sample of the substance was submitted to a private lab and they were unable to analyze the substance due to the fact that it disappeared or disintegrated. Skin samples were analyzed by the State Police Lab and the Medical Examiner's Office. It was reported that the skin had been cut with a sharp instrument.

Three days later, Officer Valdez was quietly speaking with people from Sandia Nation Laboratories, whose work revolves around nuclear technology, much of it undertaken at Kirtland Air Force Base in New Mexico. As we have seen, a team of Kirtland's intelligence agencies was deeply involved in the 1973 abduction experience of Judy Doraty— an incident which had a cattle mutilation aspect attached to it. Valdez convinced Sandia's Dr. Howard Burgess to come out to the site of the latest mute—which Burgess did. He found abnormal radiation levels in the very areas where the strange tripod marks had been discovered. But there was more to come: the mutilators were soon back, to the very same site, incredibly. On this issue, Valdez wrote, "There was also evidence that the tripod marks had returned and removed the left ear. Tripod marks were found over Mr. Gomez's tire tracks of his original visit. The left ear was intact when Mr. Gomez first found the cow. The cow had a 3-month-old calf which has not been located since the incident. This appears strange since a small calf normally stays around the mother even though the cow is dead."

Theories Abound

It's not at all surprising Valdez concluded that none of this was the work of coyotes, scavengers, or even satanic cults, the latter being a thought-provoking theory which was mooted for awhile. On the matter of the attacks being the work of cultists or wild animals, Valdez had this to say:

Both have been ruled out due to expertise and preciseness and the cost involved to conduct such a sophisticated and secretive operation. It should also be noted that during the spring of 1974 when a tremendous amount of cattle were lost due to heavy snowfalls, the carcasses had been eaten by predators. These carcasses did not resemble the carcasses of the mutilated cows. Investigation has narrowed down to these theories which involve (1) Experimental use of Vitamin B12 and (2) The testing of the lymph node system. During this investigation an intensive study has been made of (3) What is involved in germ warfare testing, and the possible correlation of these 3 factors (germ warfare testing, use of Vitamin B12, testing of the lymph node system).

Let's now take a look at a 1978 case from Valdez, also from Arriba County, New Mexico:

This four year old cross Hereford and Black Angus native cow was found lying on left side with rectum, sex organs, tongue, and ears removed. Pinkish blood from [illegible] was visible, and after two days the blood still had not coagulated. Left front and left rear leg were pulled out of their sockets apparently from the weight of the cow which indicates that it was lifted and dropped back to the ground. The ground around and under the cow was soft and showed indentations where the cow had been dropped. 600 yards away from the cow were the 4-inch circular indentations similar to the ones found at the Manuel Gomez ranch on 4-24-78.

This cow had been dead approximately [illegible] hours and was too decomposed to extract samples. This is the first in a series of mutilations in which the cows' legs are broken. Previously the animals had been lifted from the brisket with a strap. These mutilated animals all dehydrate rapidly (in one or two days).

"Boundless Financing and Secrecy"

A further case caught the attention of Valdez. It too occurred in 1978, at the height of the summer. He recorded the following:

It is believed that this type of radiation is not harmful to humans, although approximately 7 people who visited the mutilation site complained of nausea and headaches. However, this writer has had no such symptoms after checking approximately 11 mutilations in the past 4 months. Identical mutilations have been taking place all over the Southwest. It is strange that no eye witnesses have come forward or that no accidents occurred. One has to admit that whoever is responsible for the mutilations is very well organized with boundless financing and secrecy. Writer is presently getting equipment through the efforts of Mr. Howard Burgess, Albuquerque, N.M. to detect substances on the cattle which might mark them and be picked up by infra-red rays but not visible to the naked eye.

Of the various people in the FBI who received Officer Valdez's files, one was a man named Forrest S. Putman, who ran the FBI office in Albuquerque, New Mexico. Putman—who died in 2015—was both impressed and puzzled by what Valdez's files revealed. He made a point to share a summary report with numerous sources within his organization.

It read:

Information furnished to this office by Officer Valdez indicates that the animals are being shot with some type of paralyzing drug and the blood is being drawn from the animal after an injection of an anti-coagulant. It appears that in some instances the cattle's legs have been broken and helicopters without any identifying numbers have reportedly been seen in the vicinity of these mutilations [italics mine].

> *Officer Valdez theorizes that clamps are being placed on the cow's legs and they are being lifted by helicopter to some remote area where the mutilations are taking place and then the animal is returned to its original pasture [italics mine]. The mutilations primarily consist of removal of the tongue, the lymph gland, lower lip and the sexual organs of the animal.*

Much mystery has surrounded these mutilations, but according to witnesses they give the appearance of being very professionally done with a surgical instrument, and according to Valdez, as the years progress, each surgical procedure appears to be more professional. Officer Valdez has advised that in no instance, to his knowledge, are these carcasses ever attacked by predator or scavenger animals, although there are tracks which would indicate that coyotes have been circling the carcass from a distance. Special Agent Putman then informed the director of the outcome of Valdez's run-ins with officials: "He also advised that he has requested Los Alamos Scientific Laboratory to conduct investigation for him but until just recently has always been advised that the mutilations were done by predatory animals. Officer Valdez stated that just recently he has been told by two assistants at Los Alamos Scientific Laboratory that they were able to determine the type of tranquilizer and blood anti-coagulant that have been utilized."

The above document is highly important: note that although Officer Valdez was of the opinion that the helicopter crews were the real sources of the attacks, he recorded something which echoes back to the Judy Doraty alien abduction incident of 1973. Valdez had concluded that the cattle were taken into the sky, mutilated, and then dropped back to the place they were first taken from. This is *exactly* what Judy Doraty described: an animal taken onboard a craft, quickly sliced and diced, and then dropped back into the pasture. The only difference was that Valdez thought this was all the work of a clandestine group within the US government (and using helicopters, black or otherwise), whereas Doraty was sure it was all the work of aliens.

Putman added:

Officer Valdez stated that Colorado probably has the most mutilations occurring within their State and that over the past four years approximately 30 have occurred in New Mexico. He stated that of these 30, 15 have occurred on Indian Reservations but he did know that many mutilations have gone unreported which have occurred on the Indian reservations because the Indians, particularly in the Pueblos, are extremely superstitious and will not even allow officers in to investigate in some instances. Officer Valdez stated since the outset of these mutilations there have been an estimated 8,000 animals mutilated which would place the loss at approximately $1,000,000.

Despite all of this clear evidence that something undeniably bizarre and widespread was taking place, the only action the FBI took was to bring a retired FBI special agent on board to look into the matter, Kenneth M. Rommel Jr. With a grant from the Law Enforcement Assistance Administration, Rommel and his small team concluded, in 1980, that the whole thing was the work of predators. And nothing else. The door was quickly and forever closed by the FBI on both mysteries: the cattle mutilations and the black helicopters. And all too conveniently, many thought, including Officer Gabe Valdez.

13 MYSTERIOUS HELICOPTERS, UFOS, AND ABDUCTIONS

t's time, now, to demonstrate deep connections between the black heli-copters and UFO activity—which includes alien abductions. When, in 1975, cattle mutilations were reported across much of the United States, reports of UFO encounters were at their height. On top of that, those mysterious helicopters were watching that same UFO activity—and very carefully, too. Declassified US Air Force files on the 1975 incidents make a very good case that a veritable UFO invasion was going on—an invasion that was primarily targeting military installations.

An Air Force report of 1975, with the eye-catching title of "Suspicious Unknown Air Activity," states:

Since 28 Oct 75 numerous reports of suspicious objects have been received at the NORAD CC. Reliable military personnel at Loring AFB, Maine, Wurtsmith AFB, Michigan, Malmstrom AFB, MT, Minot AFB, ND, and Canadian forces station Falconbridge, Ontario Canada have visually sighted suspicious objects. Objects at Loring and Wurtsmith were characterized to be helicopters. Missile site personnel, security alert teams and air defense personnel at Malmstrom, Montana report an object which sounded like a jet. FAA advised there were no jet aircraft in the vicinity. Malmstrom search and height finder radars carried the object between 9500 ft. and 15,000 ft. at a speed of seven knots. Personnel reported the object as low as 200 ft. and said that as the interceptors approached the lights went out, after the interceptors had passed the lights came on again. Minot AFB on 10 Nov reported that the site was buzzed by a bright object the size of a car at an altitude of 1,000 to 2,000 ft. There was no noise emitted by the vehicle.

An officer whose name has been erased from the available files said the following in an official memorandum: "Be assured that this command is doing everything possible to identify and provide solid factual information on these sightings. I have also expressed my concern to SAFOI that we come up soonest with a proposed answer to queries from the press to prevent over reaction by the public to reports by the media that may be blown out of proportion. To date efforts by Air Guard helicopters, SAC helicopters and NORAD F106s have failed to produce positive ID."

"An Unidentified Helicopter Has Been Observed"

Things got even more intriguing when some of the military facilities whose staff reported UFO incidents soon had something else to deal with: unmarked helicopters flying the skies by night and checking out the very locations where the UFOs were seen only a few nights earlier. This is demonstrated perfectly in an official Air Force report headed "Defense Against Helicopter Assault." It states: "The past two evenings at one of our northern tier bases, an unidentified helicopter has been observed hovering over and in the near vicinity of the weapons storage area. Attempts to identify this aircraft have so far met with negative results."

A nearly identical story is told in yet another Air Force document, this one captioned "Unidentified Helicopter Sighted at Low Level Over Loring AFB." The file is lengthy, but a couple particular extracts will make the point:

On 28 Oct 75, Lewis . . . advised that the a/c [aircraft] was first observed by Clifton W. Blakeslee, Sgt. [deleted] and William J. Long, Sgt., both assigned to the 42 SPS, who were on duty at the storage area. The initial sighting took place at approximately 1345. The a/c was observed approximately 1,000 meters north of LAFB. The a/c was subsequently observed by Lewis and others intermittently for the next hour and a half. Subsequent to the sighting by Long and Blakeslee, the a/c did not come nearer to the northern perimeter of LAFB than approximately 3 miles. Lewis observed a flashing white strobe light and red navigation lights on the a/c. The operator of the a/c either turned the lights off periodically or the a/c flew below a point from which the lights could be observed. The a/c disappeared from view and did not reappear. A search of the vicinity of the northern perimeter of LAFB by 42 SPS personnel met with negative results.

The mysterious matter unfolded even further:

On 28 Oct 75, Commander, 42 8W, advised that he responded to the area from which the unidentified a/c was observed. He arrived at approximately 1955. The a/c bore a white flashing light and an amber or orange light. The speed and movement in the air suggested that the a/c was a helicopter *[emphasis mine]. From 1345-2020, the a/c was under constant observation. Subsequent to that time the a/c would appear and disappear from view. The a/c definitely penetrated the LAFB northern perimeter and on one occasion was within 300 yards of the munitions storage area perimeter. Efforts to identify the a/c through Maine State Police and local police departments were not successful.*

Like so many UFO encounters referenced in the pages of this book, the mysterious events of 1975 were never resolved to the satisfaction of the military and the intelligence community.

"The Object Appeared as a 100 Ft. Diameter Sphere"

On November 7, 1975, Malmstrom Air Force Base was experiencing strange aerial activity in the morning hours: "Received a call from the 341st Strategic Air Command Post, saying that the following missile locations reported seeing a large red to orange to yellow object: M-1, L-3, LIMA and L-6. The general object location would be 10 miles south of Moore, Montana and 20 miles east of Buffalo, Montana."

Then, shortly after one in the afternoon, the following was logged: "SAC advised K-1 says very bright object to their east is now southeast of them and they are looking at it with 10 x 50 binoculars. Object seems to have lights (several) on it, but no distinct pattern. The orange/gold object overhead also has small lights on it. SAC also advises female civilian reports having seen an object bearing south from her position six miles west of Lewsitown."

The North American Air Defense Command (NORAD) was hit too by the wave of mysterious intrusions. Its staff reported the following: "This morning, 11 Nov 75, CFS Falconbridge reported search and height finder radar paints on an object up to 30 nautical miles south of the site ranging in altitude from 26,000 to 72,000 feet. The site commander and other personnel say the object appeared as a bright star but much closer. With binoculars the object appeared as a 100 ft. diameter sphere and appeared to have craters around the outside."

The above material is just the tip of the iceberg. Hundreds of pages of formerly classified files on the UFO–helicopter wave of 1975 are now in the public domain. When studied carefully, it makes a very strong case that when UFOs intruded upon sensitive military installations, the black helicopters were never far behind.

It should be noted, too, that this particular period—November 1975—was the same time frame in which one of the most famous of all alien abductions on record occurred. The victim was a man named Travis Walton, a logger kidnapped by alien beings from Arizona's Sitgreaves National Forest on November 5. Walton was gone for five days, during which he was subjected to the typically intrusive experiments that are the typical calling cards of the Greys. Now, we'll see how the crews of the black helicopters have—in the last couple of decades—increased their surveillance of alien abductees.

Spying in the Skies

Betty Andreasson is a well-known alien abductee whose incredible encounters with extraterrestrial creatures—which began in 1967—have been chronicled in numerous books by UFO investigator Raymond Fowler, including *The Andreasson Affair, The Andreasson Affair—Phase Two*, and *The Andreasson Legacy*. That Andreasson has been the subject of a number of books makes it not at all surprising that there should be a government file on her. This possibility is made all the more likely by the fact that she and her husband, Bob Luca, have had more than a few run-ins with the black helicopters. UFO researchers Barry Greenwood and Lawrence Fawcett took a particular interest in the helicopter encounters that Betty and Bob reported.

Greenwood and Fawcett said the husband and wife "reported that their home was over flown numerous times by black, unmarked helicopters of the Huey UH-1H type and that these helicopters would fly over their homes at altitudes as low as 100 feet. The Lucas described these helicopters as being black in color, with no identifiable marking on them. They noticed that the windows were tinted black also, so that no one could see inside. During many of the over flights, Bob was able to take close to 200 photos of the helicopters."

Raymond Fowler, who faithfully chronicled the saga of Betty and Bob, revealed something intriguing on this matter, too: "Bob Luca became obsessed with tracking down the strange helicopters that harassed them at home and on the road. But to date, Bob has been able to identify only one of the helicopters involved in the overflights. He tracked it back to Sikorsky Aircraft. The control tower told him that it was probably a 'Navy Blackhawk aircraft flown by a military acceptance crew.' Bob fired back a letter to Sikorsky and complained not only about their contradictory identification but also that the aircraft had no identification markings and flew dangerously low over his house."

It was then a case of passing the buck, for national security reasons.

There are other examples of the secret surveillance Bob and Betty have had to endure. In 1988, Bob was quoted in *Connecticut Magazine*: "I have no doubt that our phone was tapped. I bought a device that is supposed to detect a tap, and it lit up for our phone but not for one of the others I tested it on."

Betty too had a strange experience along the same lines: "Once I picked [the phone] up to make an outgoing call and a voice on the other end said 'director's office.' I asked 'director of what?' and the person got all excited and said, 'Oh, I'm sorry,' and hung up."

The List Goes On

Alien abductee Debbie Jordan has experienced treatment similar to Bob Luca and Betty Andreasson. She says of the unmarked helicopters she has encountered:

These could be seen almost daily around our houses. They are so obvious about their flights it's almost comical. On occasions too numerous to even remember, they have hovered around my house, above my house, and above me for several minutes at a time, not trying to hide themselves or the fact that they are watching us.

Even when I am outside and obviously watching back, it doesn't seem to bother them. They just sit there in midair, about sixty to ninety feet above the ground, whirling and watching. They are completely without identification and are always low enough so that I could easily see the pilot, if the windshield were clear glass. But the windshield is smoky black, with a finish that makes it impossible to see who's inside.

In a later chapter, we'll see how the mysterious helicopters have even impacted Whitley Strieber, whose 1987 book on his own abductions, *Communion*, brought the phenomenon to a massive new audience.

While large questions remain regarding who is flying the helicopters and where they originate from, longtime ufologist Tommy Blann has a few ideas. A contact in the US Army informed Blann that all across the United States, there are "underground installations, as well as isolated areas of military reservations [which] have squadrons of unmarked helicopters, which have sophisticated instrumentation on board, that are dispatched to areas of UFO activity to monitor these craft or airlift them out of the area if one has malfunctioned."

14 NIGHTMARES UNDER NEW MEXICO

I s it possible the US government is hiding a terrible secret about the alien abduction phenomenon? Just about the worst secret possible? Namely, that there exists a huge underground installation far below the remote New Mexican town of Dulce, to which alien abductees are taken . . . but never returned? It sounds like bizarre, over-the-top science fiction. But what if it isn't? What if it's true—and maybe even worse than we know or suspect? Welcome to the world of what has become known as the Dulce base, after the aforementioned town under which it allegedly exists.

At first glance, there doesn't seem to be anything unusual about Dulce in the slightest. It's a small locale of fewer than three thousand people, the majority of them being Native American. Home to the tribal headquarters of the Jicarilla Apache Reservation, the town dates back to 1887, when it was first settled. It has an inviting landscape and is dominated by hills, trees, and green slopes. And the pace of life is far removed from that of the average bustling city. It's a perfect environment for those who have no time for the rat race, except for one thing: the alleged atrocities going on below the town's vast Archuleta Mesa.

UFO researchers talk about huge numbers of alien abductees being held against their will in a giant facility thousands of feet below the surface and, in some cases, used in genetic experiments. There are even claims they have been used for food. The government, the rumor mill goes, is unable to do anything about it. The military is helpless: trying to destroy the base would possibly reveal the bleak truth to the public and the media, something which might create even more chaos and fear than already exists. So the government stays as far away as it can from the base, hoping that the abductors from the stars will one day leave—and leave for good. But, how did this strange and almost unbelievable saga begin? Why do so many people in ufology believe that such a base exists? It all revolves around a man named Paul Bennewitz.

A Scientist Fears an Alien Takeover

As far back as the 1960s, Paul Bennewitz had an interest in UFOs. He was a card-carrying member of the Arizona-based Aerial Phenomena Research Organization (APRO), and he and his wife, Cindy, lived in a pleasant part of Albuquerque, New Mexico. The offices of his company, Thunder Scientific, backed onto Kirtland Air Force Base—a facility which would come to play a significant role in the Dulce story.

Given that the Bennewitz family lived in Albuquerque, and taking into consideration Bennewitz's long-standing interest in UFOs, it's not at all surprising that Bennewitz took great interest in the cattle mutilation phenomenon which had hit various parts of New Mexico in the mid- to late 1970s. And he quickly took note when, in 1979, he started to see strange aerial vehicles flying silently across the skies of Kirtland. He was sure they weren't helicopters. And they definitely weren't regular aircraft. For Bennewitz, this left just one answer available: UFOs. But what were alien spaceships doing flying over the base and the huge Sandia Mountains nearby in the dead of night? In the early days of his investigations, and when his mind was largely free of the paranoia that later overwhelmed him, Bennewitz suspected that aliens were just checking out what was going on at Kirtland. Within no time at all, however, and when he was exposed to the horror stories coming out of Dulce, Bennewitz came to think that some faction of the military had been invited to work hand-in-glove with dangerous ETs—one of those Mafia-style offers it's never wise to refuse.

As a result of his growing suspicions that the aliens and the military were in some kind of reckless cahoots, Bennewitz did something that proved to be his downfall: he approached staff at Kirtland and told them all about his research into the strange craft flying over the base and the mountains. He shared with them recordings of strange transmissions that came through his radio equipment, which he believed were coded alien messages, and admitted that he suspected there was something dangerous and disturbing going on in New Mexico—maybe even a secretly planned invasion of our planet by a gigantic alien armada.

The military and intelligence officers Bennewitz spoke with listened carefully. Whatever the true nature and origin of those craft and signals, the people at Kirtland were highly concerned by the fact that Bennewitz was onto . . . well, onto something. They wanted to know exactly what Bennewitz knew. Hardly surprisingly, he was placed under intense surveillance: his home was watched, his phones—both at home and at work—were tapped, and on occasion his mail was intercepted and read. Bennewitz soon found himself caught up in a bizarre world filled with truths, half-truths, lies, and half-lies concerning alien abductions and extraterrestrial visitation—and to the point that he didn't know what the truth was. The outcome: he finally went off the rails. But before we get to that, we need to take a strange detour in the story of Paul Bennewitz.

Bennewitz Is Exposed to the Alien Abduction Enigma

There's no doubt that matters really went into high gear when Paul Bennewitz was introduced to a woman named Myrna Hansen. On May 6, 1980, a panicky Hansen phoned the Cimarron Police Department in New Mexico with a confusing tale of something strange that had happened to her fewer than twenty-four hours earlier. As a result of her frantic, almost hysterical state of mind, Hansen didn't make much sense. All the officer on the other end of the line could make out were references to mysterious lights in the sky, people who may not have been people after all, and cattle. As luck would have it, though, the officer knew none other than Officer Gabe Valdez—who, as we have seen, played a significant role in the 1970s-era investigations into cattle mutilations, black helicopters, and alien abductions. It just so happens that Bennewitz and Valdez had become friends—after meeting at an April 20, 1979, cattle mutilation conference at the Albuquerque Public Library; it was a conference which was packed with undercover intelligence personnel from Kirtland and special agents of the FBI. And, due to the Valdez–Bennewitz connection, it wasn't long at all before the latter found himself deep in the heart of the Myrna Hansen saga.

Valdez put in a call to the Cimarron police and asked if one of their officers could drive Hansen the approximately two hundred miles to Bennewitz's home in Albuquerque. Fortunately, one of the officers was able to do just that, and as a result, Bennewitz and Hansen were soon brought together and the investigation of the latter's astonishing experience began. And "astonishing" is not an exaggeration.

Cattle and a Close Encounter

On the night of May 5, 1980, Hansen and her young son were driving through northeastern New Mexico when they saw something strange in the sky. Actually, two things: a giant UFO, bigger than a pair of Goodyear blimps put together, and a triangular-shaped object of smaller dimensions. But that's when things became somewhat confusing.

Although the welcoming atmosphere in the Bennewitz home helped to calm Hansen down, it was if a door had been placed in her mind—through this door was the most fantastic part of the story, but she was unable to pass through it. Bennewitz contacted Jim Lorenzen of the Aerial Phenomena Research Organization (APRO) and asked if he had any suggestions for how they might try to figure out what really happened to Hansen and her son. As it happens, Lorenzen *did* have an idea: he suggested bringing in Leo Sprinkle—who, remember, was instrumental to unveiling the curtains Judy Doraty's mind, who had witnessed a horrifying cattle mutilation event in 1973.

Sprinkle booked a flight and was in Albuquerque on the eleventh. He wasted no time in hypnotizing Hansen. The contents of that hypnotic session make for both absorbing and troubling reading. Now released publicly, the contents include the following from Hansen on that nightmarish evening:

I'm driving. My son's right there in my car, talking to me. I'm half tuning him out. The light is so bright. I feel like it's coming in on me. I stop the car and we get out. This isn't real. It can't be happening. What is it? There's another one. The bright is confusing. I want to leave, but I want to see what it is. My son wants to leave, but I've got to know what's going on. So much commotion. They're landing. Oh, God! Cattle are screaming! But I've got to know who is . . . the light is so bright. It's orange. I want to see them. I want to go to them. I'm out of the car. Screaming of the cattle. It's horrible, it's horrible! Incredible pain! I still want to get to them, but they're mad.

The hypnosis also revealed that a significant number of hours had been lost during the Hansen's trip from Oklahoma to Eagle's Nest, New Mexico. She was also able to recall seeing a cow somehow being sucked into one of the craft—it was almost identical to the Judy Doraty incident of 1973. The story got even more bizarre and sinister: while still under hypnosis, Hansen described being taken to a belowground facility, where she saw body parts in "vat"-like containers. She also recalled being implanted with a tiny device—but for what purpose she didn't know. Bennewitz believed the implant would allow the aliens to monitor not just her movements, but her thoughts too. It's perhaps not surprising that the Air Force was soon on the case—just as they were with the Judy Doraty saga of seven years earlier.

The Military and the Issue of Implants

Bennewitz was in touch with various players from Kirtland Air Force Base: chiefly, intelligence agents and military officers. When he confided in them the facts surrounding Myrna Hansen's jarring encounter, they sat up and took notice big-time. The Air Force even quietly arranged for Hansen to meet with personnel from the New Mexico–based Lovelace Medical Center. There was a good reason for that: staff from the facility had been involved in studying the cattle population in northern New Mexico—cattle which may have been exposed to radiation under mysterious circumstances. On top of that, the Lovelace facility had a building on Kirtland Air Force Base.

Hansen was taken to the Lovelace installation—on three occasions—and x-rayed. The military wanted to know if that implant Hansen had talked about was real. Greg Bishop says the military was determined to find out if they could locate the minute device which "Bennewitz was sure was embedded near the base of her skull along the spinal cord." Sure enough, something *was* seen—but Air Force doctors confided in Bennewitz that it was nothing more than a "natural growth." Whether those same doctors were telling the truth or trying to keep Bennewitz from learning that aliens really *were* secretly implanting American citizens with unknown devices and for unknown purposes remains unknown.

The story wasn't quite over, though: further digging into the matter of that underground facility to which Hansen was taken went ahead—this time by the Air Force, rather than Bennewitz. Hansen was soon hypnotized by a psychologist at Kirtland Air Force Base, which led to an incredible revelation. In her hypnotized state, Hansen described being taken to what was without a doubt one of the most secure underground facilities at Kirtland—a weapons-storage area that was comprised of several below-surface levels. No one could explain how Hansen could have described the area unless she had personally been there. It's hardly surprising, then, that all of this sent Bennewitz's fear-filled paranoia through the roof: he now suspected, to his horror, that the military was indeed working with the aliens on a top-secret program that involved alien abductions and cattle mutilations. He even suspected that portions of the underground Kirtland base may have been handed over to the extraterrestrial invaders. By force or willingly, he didn't know.

Alien implants, cattle killed and dissected by strangers from the skies, abductees taken underground on a military base, the Air Force hypnotizing Hansen—what the hell was going on? Bennewitz knew he had to continue to dig further still. He did exactly that—ultimately, to his cost and to his health.

For Bennewitz, the Picture Comes Together

As Bennewitz began to piece the story together—a thesis he called Project Beta—he was approached by shadowy figures from Kirtland who advised him that if he wanted the *real* scoop on what was going down, then he really should turn away from Kirtland and focus his attention on the small northern town of Dulce. It was then that Bennewitz was exposed to the entire horrific story. It was clear that Bennewitz was onto something— something big—but what? Had Bennewitz come across a highly classified military program at Kirtland? If so, was he diverted to Dulce as a means to keep him away from whatever it was that was going on at Kirtland? Or, incredibly, did the military and the intelligence community choose to confide in Bennewitz a *real* story of aliens under Dulce and kidnapped citizens? Could it have been a bit of both? Maybe.

Whatever the truth was, when Bennewitz received horror story upon horror story of abductees being eaten by aliens or used in terrible experiments, and of men, women, and children being implanted with what he was told by military personnel were mind-controlling devices, Bennewitz's lid was well and truly flipped. Big-time, too. His paranoia increased, as did his stress levels. He couldn't sleep, which affected his ability to work at Thunder Scientific. Exhaustion soon set in—as did, finally, a complete breakdown. Bennewitz was checked into a medical center for treatment. He was a shell of his former self, a man burdened by just about the worst secret possible. Fortunately, Bennewitz made a recovery, but he was never quite the same again: his state of mind was still somewhat fragile and he shunned the

UFO research community, preferring to keep his research to himself. He died in the summer of 2003, in Albuquerque, at the age of seventy-five. He never knew for sure what the truth was about UFOs, alien abductions, and the Dulce base. But others followed Bennewitz, all of them determined to uncover the truth.

Dulce: A Mystery-Filled Town

Such is the amazing and controversial nature of the story of the Dulce base that it's not at all surprising the story didn't die when Bennewitz walked away from it. In fact, an entire subculture quickly came into being, which is still intact today. One of the most intriguing and thought-provoking things about the town of Dulce is that it really does have a long history of high-strangeness firmly attached to it dating back to the 1960s. That was when the area was chosen by the Atomic Energy Commission (AEC) to be the site of a controversy-filled experiment.

The operation was known as Gasbuggy, a subproject of a larger program with the codename Plowshare. The AEC had an ambitious idea to detonate a small atomic device under Carson National Forest, which covers more than 1.5 million acres of northern New Mexico. Incredibly, the detonation was not just a plan: it came to fruition on December 10, 1967. The goal was to secure valuable pockets of natural gas by literally blasting through the ground, which is exactly what happened.

Today, however, more than a few UFO researchers believe that the detonation was not to try to locate natural gas pockets, but to destroy the underground base at Dulce. That the town is, admittedly, only a few miles from Carson National Forest has only increased suspicions that one secret operation acted as a cover for another. And it's a fact that digging in the area is still strictly forbidden today by stringent federal laws. No wonder, then, that the story of the Dulce base has turned a few skeptics into full-blown believers. Then, just before the dawning of the 1990s, the FBI released into the public domain its files on cattle mutilations in and around Dulce—files that ran to around 150 packed pages and included the vitally important papers of Officer Gabe Valdez.

Now, the time has come to take a look at the wildest claim of all: that way below Dulce's Archuleta Mesa, countless masses of alien abductees are transformed into nourishment for the aliens—and although the government secretly knows this, it's helpless to stop it.

Secret Levels and Evil Experiments

One source of the Dulce stories was a man who used the alias Tal Lavesque. He claimed, in the pages of a highly controversial report called *The Dulce Papers*, that he had spoken to a military man who had successfully managed to penetrate certain parts of the base. That man was said to have been named Thomas Castello. Castello reportedly said this of the multilevel underground facility:

Level 7 is worse, row after row of thousands of humans and human mixtures in cold storage. Here too are embryo storage vats of humanoids in various stages of development. I frequently encountered humans in cages, usually dazed or drugged, but sometimes they cried and begged for help. We were told they were hopelessly insane, and involved in high risk drug tests to cure insanity. We were told to never try to speak to them at all. At the beginning we believed that story. Finally in 1978 a small group of workers discovered the truth.

Alan B. de Walton is the author of *The Dulce Book*, a long and winding publication written under the alias "Branton." One of de Walton's sources said that we, humans, are "surrounded by the etheric 'body,' surrounded by the astral 'body,' surrounded by the mental 'body.'" He continued, "We also actually have an extra 'body,' the emotional 'body,' that the aliens don't have. This part of us constantly puts out a kind of energy they cannot generate or simulate. This emotional energy . . . is to them, like a potent, much sought-after drug. They can take it out of us and bottle it, so to speak. . . . Also during this 'harvesting,' Greys will look directly into our eyes, as if they are drinking something or basking in light."

A further source reported seeing "a vat full of red liquid and body parts of humans and animals . . . she could see Greys bobbing up and down, almost swimming." This is very similar to what Myrna Hansen reported seeing: "body-parts in 'vat'-like containers."

Researcher and author Joshua Cutchin has offered his thoughts on this particularly inflammatory issue: "While abduction research does not overtly suggest that aliens are harvesting people for consumption, there may be a grain of truth to the report [contained in the pages of Valerian's *Matrix II*]. 'Nourishment is ingested by smearing a soupy mixture of biologicals on the epidermis. Food sources include Bovine cattle and human parts . . . distilled into a high protein broth.'"

Then there is David Jacobs, who penned *The Threat* and *Walking Among Us*. He suspects that "aliens obtain fuel differently from humans, that their skin has a very unique function, and that they convert 'food' to energy very differently." Jacobs makes another important point on this issue: "But these are mere glimpses into alien life and biology, and the reason we do not know more is that the aliens do not want us to know."

US Army Colonel Philip J. Corso, the coauthor with William J. Birnes of *The Day After Roswell*, speculated on something very similar. He said that "if an exchange of nutrients and waste occurred within their systems, that exchange could only have taken place through the creature's skin or the outer protective covering they wore because there were no digestive or waste systems."

Paul Bennewitz is long gone. Those intelligence-based and military personnel at Kirtland Air Force Base, who fed the Dulce tale to Bennewitz, are either dead or in retirement. They are saying nothing. But the story of the Dulce base and its imprisoned (and possibly eaten or absorbed) alien abductees lives on. Whether the story is true, though, is quite another matter. Sometimes, fact really is stranger than fiction. On the other hand, though, fiction is sometimes presented as fact to hide another truth.

Somewhere, and somehow, the saga of Paul Bennewitz falls into one of these categories. Possibly even in a confusing, chaotic collage of both.

Military Mind Control and an Abductee

Another individual who found himself being watched—and watched closely—by military intelligence in the same time frame that Paul Bennewitz was researching government surveillance of alien abductees was a man named Conrad Zerbe. Although not a well-known figure in the field of ufology, Zerbe had a strange and illuminating story to tell. It was a story that has its origins in none other than ufology's number one case: Roswell.

It was back in early July 1947 that an object crashed to the ground on a remote ranch in Lincoln County, New Mexico, which is about a ninety-minute drive from Roswell. Although the Roswell affair is seen by most ufologists as the most important case of all time, it's a fact that numerous theories have been put forward for what, exactly, came down on that fateful day. They include—obviously—a spacecraft from another world. Other possibilities include a secret device of the military with a crew of human guinea pigs used in high-altitude exposure experiments; and an advanced craft of the Russians. Even time travelers have been suggested as good candidates. And that's just a few of the now more than twelve theories for all the fuss.

What we know for sure is that the military from Roswell quickly descended on the ranch, ensuring that no one was allowed on the property. The rancher there was warned never to talk about what was seen and found. Death threats were made to local people who had seen the wreckage and several strange, small bodies before the military managed to get there. As a result of the silencing, the case vanished into almost complete oblivion. That is, until the mid- to late 1970s, when two ufologists, Bill Moore and Stanton Friedman, began digging into the story. As a result, hundreds of people were tracked down, many of them in old age by then and ready to talk. The floodgates were about to open.

Roswell has now been the subject of dozens of books, a movie, and several investigations by the government, specifically the US Air Force and the Government Accountability Office. The official line is that the unusual wreckage found on the ranch came from a huge military balloon array. As for the bodies? The military maintains they were crash test dummies used in parachute experiments. Ufologists roll their eyes at such claims. Now, back to Conrad Zerbe.

A Man with a Mountain of Secrets

Someone whose story has gone well under the radar of most Roswell researchers, Conrad Zerbe played a notable role in the Roswell affair. Whatever it was that plummeted onto the ranch, Zerbe saw it all. There is a very good reason for that: he was an integral part of a team brought in to photograph and film the site, and to chronicle just about every aspect of the affair on film. Zerbe died in 1992 and his remains are buried in California's San Joaquin National Cemetery. In the 1980s, however, he revealed portions of what he knew about Roswell—and his role in it, too.

It was in 1980 that Charles Berlitz and Bill Moore's book on the crash, *The Roswell Incident*, was published. When word got out in the world of ufology that the book was due to surface, word also got back to Zerbe—who thought now might be the time to reveal what he knew. The story was an extraordinary one.

According to Zerbe, his photographic team was comprised of a Colonel Loomis, a Captain Edward Guill, Roland S. Cliff, whose rank Zerbe could not remember, and a civilian attached to one of the intelligence agencies—possibly the CIA, which was created in 1947—whose name was Bohanon. The entire team was at the site filming and shooting the debris and photographing the badly damaged bodies, which were rapidly decomposing under New Mexico's hot summer sun. It was made abundantly clear to everyone that silence was the name of the game. The alternatives didn't even bear thinking about.

126

According to Zerbe, while he and his team were out at the crash site, they experienced a period of what in alien abduction terminology has become known as missing time. Having kept up with the UFO journals and books of the day, he strongly came to believe that aliens had abducted him and his comrades from the ranch for at least several hours early on the second morning of the incident and experimented on him (something which he did not expand upon). Now, in 1980, it was time for Zerbe to blow the lid off. Surely, after all those years, the US government wouldn't still be watching him, would they? Well, as it happens, yes, they would.

Drugged and Interrogated—All in the Name of National Security

It was on one particular morning in the latter part of 1980 that Zerbe got a knock on the door of his small apartment in a rundown block in Los Angeles. He opened the door to a man dressed in a smart suit and with what looked like a classic military crew cut. The man's air and approach clinched it. So did the Air Force ID he thrust in Zerbe's worried face. More than thirty years after the events of the summer of 1947, the Air Force wanted to talk again. Zerbe invited him in. Warily, it must be stressed.

Probably deducing that Zerbe was worried by the sudden arrival of the Man, he told Zerbe that he was not in any trouble—chiefly because he hadn't done anything wrong. At least, not yet, he hadn't. And that's how the Air Force wanted it: no loose lips and no telling his story to the press or the UFO research community. The Air Force guy, Zerbe couldn't fail to note, arrived with a couple of sodas. The pair sat opposite each other, Zerbe in a recliner and the man on Zerbe's couch. The mysterious man passed Zerbe a soda, and Zerbe proceeded to chug it. In just a few minutes, he began to feel weird, spaced out. When the man then asked what he, Zerbe, had been doing for the last few years, Zerbe found himself almost babbling, talking all about his life and—when prompted—what happened at Roswell, including the missing time angle, which the Air Force man seemed particularly intrigued by.

There then followed *another* period of missing time: half an hour, or thereabouts, had seemingly passed and the officer was gone. Zerbe, still a bit groggy, but with his mind back to normal, was now in a state of fear: the military had drugged and questioned him to make sure they knew all about his role in Roswell. After all those years, the Air Force was still watching Zerbe, still waiting for the day when he decided to reveal all about the events at Roswell, and the nature of the old photos and film footage. And, of course, that period of missing time on the ranch, which Zerbe suspected had been a full-blown abduction by aliens. Probably, he thought, by the comrades of the dead aliens who lost their lives in the high-speed crash.

In light of that fateful day, Zerbe—suspecting probably correctly that his phone was monitored—chose to hardly ever talk about the events again, living out his lonely life in a flophouse as a full-blown alcoholic; a man carrying the weight of the world on his shoulders until 1992, when the full story of what happened to him was taken to the grave.

15 AN ENCOUNTER ON THE MOORS

Imagine the scene: it's early one cold winter morning in the north of England. You are walking across a wild stretch of ancient moorland when the sight of something both incredible and terrifying catches your attention—a dwarfish creature striding along the old landscape. For a moment or two, you freeze. Then you remember you have a camera with you. Wasting no time, you quickly snap a picture of the unearthly thing, right before it vanishes. Panicked and amazed, you exit the area at high speed. But that's not the end of it. In the days ahead, you are hassled by none other than the British Ministry of Defense: they open a file on you and even dispatch a couple of Men in Black to intimidate you into silence. And as time progresses, you realize that you may have been abducted by aliens and subjected to the now-familiar missing time phenomenon.

This may all sound like the plot of some unlikely conspiracy-driven saga of fictional and sensational proportions. It's anything but. The story referred to above is nothing less than incredible fact. And it all revolved around a retired English police officer whose story sounds like it came straight out of an episode of *The X-Files*. If only it *had* been fiction.

It was December 1, 1987, when the strange affair unfolded in spectacular fashion. Because the witness held a position in the British police force, he has insisted that his real name should be kept out of the story. His identity is, however, known to a number of English UFO researchers, including Jenny Randles, Peter Hough, and me. His name was also known to the late saucer-seeker Arthur Tomlinson, who shared the intricacies of the story with me, as well as the name of the source. For the sake of privacy, though—and maybe even the witness's safety—he has been given the ID of Philip Spencer.

Three days after Spencer's incident, the mailman dropped a letter in the mailbox of UFO researcher Jenny Randles. She was used to getting UFO-themed mail from witnesses and those wanting to learn more about the subject. Today, however, was a bit different. In fact, it was a *lot* different. Randles sat down and read the contents of the letter, which turned out to be nothing less than incredible.

Catching a Creature on Film

According to Spencer's story, it was early on the morning of December 1 that he was walking across Ilkley Moor, a huge expanse of picturesque countryside in West Yorkshire, England. It very much resembles the mysterious and atmosphere-filled countryside described in Sir Arthur Conan Doyle's Sherlock Holmes novel *The Hound of the Baskervilles*. Rolling hills, massive rocks, and dense fogs are commonplace. As are tales of supernatural creatures said to haunt the area, such as fiery-eyed black dogs and ghostly apparitions. Tales of witchcraft and occult practices undertaken in the area abound. It's the perfect place for an alien or several to make an appearance.

Spencer had set out early on the morning in question, as he was due to spend time with a family relative. As a keen photographer, Spencer decided to take a few shots of the ancient rolling hills and the craggy landscape. It was as Spencer got close to the centuries-old, picturesque village of East Morton, which even today has a population of just a little more than one thousand, that reality started to unravel. With the village almost in sight, and as a fog bank rolled in, Spencer was stopped in his tracks by the sight of a small humanoid figure dark-green in color, and with a noticeably oversized head and long, thin arms, climbing amid the rocks.

The creature clearly caught sight of Spencer as it raised its hand in his direction—but whether this was a good sign or a distinctly bad one, Spencer wasn't sure. There was no time to lose: Spencer whipped out his camera and got one priceless shot which caught the creature in dead center. The whatever-it-was quickly vanished from view. Things were not quite over, though. As Spencer stood rooted to the spot, wondering what on earth had just happened, nothing less than a classic flying saucer–like craft took to the skies some distance away.

Hours Lost and a Hypnotic Session

It's hardly surprising that Spencer chose not to pay his relative a visit, but instead felt it would be far more wiser—and perhaps even safer—if he didn't hang around on a lonely stretch of moorland with no one else in sight. For Spencer, safety in numbers was very much the order of the day. He quickly headed to nearby Keighley to get the photo developed. On doing so, however, Spencer realized something strange, something very disturbing: it was close to eight in the morning when he took the picture of the mysterious dwarf, and given that the walk was not a long one, he should have been back among familiar territory in around thirty minutes. To Spencer's consternation and confusion, it was almost ten. What had happened to an approximate time of two hours? Spencer had no idea, but he was determined to find out—which is why he chose to contact Jenny Randles, who was deeply familiar with the lore and legend surrounding Ilkley Moor.

With such a sensational story, one might be inclined to suggest that Spencer was nothing but a hoaxer. Maybe even an enterprising hoaxer, one who was thinking of how much he could sell the photo for to the tabloid media. As it turned out, however, this was not the case. Spencer insisted on keeping his anonymity. He refused any and all kinds of publicity that might blow his identity far and wide. He even handed over the copyright of the photo to the aforementioned Peter Hough. This, it hardly needs saying, is not the behavior of someone who has a secret, deceptive agenda. It is, however, the behavior one might expect from a respected police officer who feared going public with a UFO story might significantly damage his future career plans. All that Spencer wanted was an answer. He got it, but it may not have been the answer he was hoping for.

Hough and Randles jumped into the controversy full-on. Checks were made of the area where the entity was seen. Hough had the presence of mind to take photos of the very spot. It was clear from Hough's photos and Spencer's that the nonhuman thing was somewhere in the region of four feet in height. There was another important issue, too, which helped to bolster Spencer's credibility. He told Hough and Randles that he had taken a number of photos of Ilkley Moor before he had that chance encounter of the incredible kind. So the pair asked Spencer for the roll of negatives. Sure enough, the negatives showed that there was just one solitary image of the assumed alien, and the rest leading up to the sensational image were indeed shots of the local landscape. Of course, had Spencer faked the picture—perhaps using a model of some sort—one would expect to see a few test shots before getting it just right. But that wasn't the case: things were just as Spencer had described them.

The saga became even more sensational when, just a few months after the early-morning encounter, Spencer agreed to a session of hypnotic regression. The delicate process was led by Jim Singleton, a respected psychologist who was skilled in the field of hypnosis, as well as unlocking the mysteries of the mind and the subconscious. What came out in the session was both incredible and disturbing. Spencer recalled that he didn't just see the alien thing, but was taken onboard a UFO (presumably the same one he saw soar into the sky), and given a "tour" of the craft. Curiously, as an aside, such tours are oddly common in such cases. Spencer was then subjected to a physical examination not unlike the ones reported by Betty and Barney Hill in 1961 and Calvin Parker and Charles Hickson in 1973. And, like so many other abductees, Spencer was shown imagery of a future worldwide Armageddon, one which would wipe out the majority of the human race and leave the Earth in ruins.

If that wasn't all enough to task the already fraught mind of Spencer, there was the matter of the Men in Black, which I have left for last.

The Government Sends Out its Agents

There's absolutely no doubt that when it came to the matter of Philip Spencer, his real identity was guarded very closely. Certainly, neither Peter Hough nor Jenny Randles have ever publicly revealed it. It was in 1999 that I was given the real name of Spencer, which was more than a decade after the encounter occurred. In that year, UFO researcher Arthur Tomlinson gave a lecture at the England-based Staffordshire UFO Group (SUFOG), which I was temporarily running, as the president of the group, Irene Bott, was getting ready to retire. Tomlinson spoke extensively about the Spencer case at the SUFOG meeting, and when it was over the two of us had a chat about the case, as Tomlinson knew I had a deep interest in the Men in Black phenomenon. He confided in me Spencer's real name, and I promised not to reveal it, which I never, ever have. Tomlinson passed away suddenly the following year.

Although barely a handful of UFO researchers ever knew Philip Spencer's real identity, it's clear that someone knew all about him and his experience—someone in the world of espionage, intelligence-gathering, and government secrecy. How the Men in Black came to know the intricacies of the affair is a mystery in itself, but that they knew all of the ins and outs is not a matter of any doubt.

Late one night, at the height of the investigation, there was a knock on the front door of the Spencer home. Spencer and his wife looked at each other, wondering who had come calling at such a late hour. They soon found out. Spencer opened the door and found himself confronted by two men dressed in suits. They both flashed ID cards, which revealed them to be from the Ministry of Defense. One was named Jefferson, the other Davies. Concerned by this new development, Spencer cautiously invited the pair in. With Spencer's wife sitting in on the chat—or maybe "interrogation" would be a better term—the MIB got straight to the point. They knew all about the encounter on Ilkley Moor, they were fully aware that Spencer had been liaising with Randles and Hough, and—as the pièce de résistance—they wanted that priceless photo. Or else. Thinking and acting quickly, Spencer said that he no longer had the picture, but stopped short of saying it was in the hands of Peter Hough. He simply said he had given it to a friend. Oddly, for what appeared to be men well-versed in the field of sensitive operations, they didn't even bother asking who the friend was. Instead, they simply stood up and exited the house, leaving Spencer and his wife concerned and confused—to the point that Spencer was close to walking away from the case and away from Randles and Hough, such were his growing concerns about the escalating affair.

There is something else, too: the MIB seemed almost transfixed by the electric fireplace in the Spencers' living room—they kept asking questions about it and seemed not to understand what it was. It must be said that such strange behavior turns up in numerous MIB cases. This has given rise to two theories: (a) that government agents deliberately act in such odd ways as a means to frighten the witnesses into believing the MIB are human-looking aliens; and (b) that they really are aliens, albeit ones that are very humanlike in appearance.

In the case of Philip Spencer, he and his wife were sure that their mysterious visitors were wholly human, but still strange and intimidating. That they knew the intricacies of the case suggests that—under circumstances that still remain unclear to this day—an extensive dossier on the incident had been compiled somewhere deep in the heart of officialdom. Predictably, when Peter Hough contacted the MoD, they denied any knowledge of such an odd visit to the home of Philip Spencer.

More than three decades after Philip Spencer had that life-changing chance encounter on Ilkley Moor, the matter still remains unsolved. As for Jefferson and Davies, they have never been seen nor heard from again. Like just about all of the MIB that have menaced UFO witnesses, they melted away into the darkness from which they came.

16 SPYING ON A BESTSELLING ABDUCTEE

The year 1987 was also notable for being the year in which the biggest-selling book on the alien abduction phenomenon—ever—was published. The author was Whitley Strieber and the book was *Communion*. Prior to writing *Communion*, Strieber was chiefly known for his horror novels, such as *The Wolfen*, *The Hunger*, and *Black Magic*. That all changed, though, in 1985, when in late December of that year Strieber had an astounding encounter of the alien abduction kind. Utterly terrified by his experience with what he called "the visitors"—but also deeply driven to find out all he could about them—Strieber began to dig into not just his own encounter but the domain of alien abductions in general. The result was an absorbing, thought-provoking, and deeply personal story of one man's personal exposure to something unearthly and almost unfathomable.

As a skilled writer, and as someone with a distinct flair for the atmospheric, Strieber was able to weave an incredible tale of how the alien abduction phenomenon radically changes lives, alters one's perceptions on reality and the world around us, and leads those exposed to the phenomenon to realize we are not alone in the universe. *Communion* was also made notable by the fact that it was quite unlike any other abduction-themed book ever published. What do I mean by that? Well, although *Communion* was certainly a study of the abduction phenomenon, it took the reader down pathways barely ever trod by other researchers of the phenomenon.

Abductions, the Human Soul, and Life after Death

Whereas the vast majority of books written on alien abduction before *Communion* were focused on the idea that aliens were using the human race as part of some bizarre, vast, and secret genetic experiment, Strieber took things much further. Off the scale, actually. Based on his own experiences, Strieber came to believe that the human soul was an integral part of the abduction experience: he concluded that the visitors had the ability to manipulate the soul, even to recycle it into newborns. Synchronicities and supernatural activity were key elements of *Communion*, as were concerns about ecological collapse, the nature of fate, and the domain of the afterlife and the dead, all weaved together in an eerie epic of almost gothic proportions.

For many researchers from the old-school, stuck-in-its-ways ufology, brought up on tales of nuts-and-bolts flying saucers and movies like *The Day the Earth Stood Still* and *Invaders from Mars*, this was something new, something radically different. Even something that many were disturbed and frightened by. Intimidated, too, maybe. Practically overnight, Strieber rewrote the alien abduction phenomenon—and in doing so, he did us all a great favor by demonstrating that there is far more to the mystery than the vast majority has ever realized.

It's hardly surprising, in light of all the above, that Strieber's book became a massive *New York Times* bestseller. And the juggernaut showed no signs of slowing down: further books followed, which told of Strieber's further experiences. They included *Transformation*, *Breakthrough*, *Confirmation*, and *The Secret School*. There was something else, too. When he was thrust into the heart of all things ufological, Strieber found that he was being watched. That's right: as the years progressed, and more and more books were published, elements of government secretly took careful notice of just about every word that came out of Strieber's keyboard.

Curious Calls and Unidentified Prowlers

In the latter part of 1992, the Strieber family started to receive disturbing late-night phone calls. Sometimes, they were way after midnight. Of course, whenever any of us gets a phone call in the early hours of the morning, we immediately assume the worst. Thankfully, they weren't those kinds of calls, but they were certainly traumatic. Typically, the voice at the other end of the line did nothing but deliver a blast of what Strieber called "scary, sneering laughter." The most obvious explanation would be that this was all the work of pranksters, or some deranged nut in ufology who had gotten hold of Strieber's private number and thought it would be fun to shake him up a bit. Maybe a lot. Except that *wasn't* the case, as Strieber was able to prove.

Quickly tired by the calls, Strieber arranged to have caller ID attached to the family's phone line. It was a very wise decision, as it revealed something remarkable. The calls were not coming from someone in ufology, after all. Rather, they were coming from a facility owned by a company called E.G. & G. Rotron. Understandably angered, and puzzled too, Strieber called them to see what was going on. He came straight to the point and told the receptionist on the line that not only had he received intimidating calls, but he had proof—via caller ID—that the calls were coming from Rotron. In other words, *take that.*

What sounded like the voice of a very old man suddenly came onto the phone and assured Strieber that he would "look into it." No further calls were made to Strieber's home, which is extremely telling. Strieber didn't stop there, though. He took on the role of detective and dug deep into the world of Rotron. In the process, he discovered that the company had ties to NASA, the Department of Energy, and even the world's most well-known secret base (which is surely the ultimate oxymoron), Area 51. Was someone at Rotron trying to destabilize Strieber with all of those late-night calls? Maybe so. That Strieber hit back—and hit back hard—quickly put paid to the psychological warfare techniques of those who were not happy with Strieber's work and the tremendous amount of exposure he had been getting since 1987. There was, however, more to come.

One year later, in 1993, after apparently being given classified information on where the US government's top-secret UFO data could be found, Strieber said, "Spooks started prowling around my neighborhood upstate. A business associate was accosted on an airplane by a group of young men who flashed badges, claimed to be with the National Security Agency, and questioned him about our activities for a couple of hours."

Those same agents were reportedly looking at attempted penetrations of Department of Defense computers. Then, on one occasion in the following year, 1994, someone managed to stealthily get into Strieber's cabin, skillfully disabling his security system in the process, and check out the contents of his computer. Clearly, Strieber was a person of deep interest to more than a few people in the shadowy world of government espionage and clandestine operations. And it wasn't just Strieber, his family, and his friends who felt the brunt of all this. There was also a man named Ed Conroy.

A Writer Gains Unwanted Attention

In 1989, Ed Conroy, a San Antonio, Texas–based journalist, wrote a book called *Report on Communion*. It was an independent study of Whitley Strieber and his incredible experiences. In taking on the project, Conroy didn't realize what he had gotten himself into. At least, not at first he didn't. What began as an impartial investigation into Strieber's claims soon mutated into something very different: Conroy found himself under intimidation similar to that which would eventually hit the Strieber family. Weird phone calls, secret surveillance, and even visits from our old friends, those mysterious black helicopters, whose crews keep more than a careful watch on alien abductees, abounded.

It was in the latter part of 1986 that Conroy was given a copy of the original manuscript of *Communion*. Initially, at least, Conroy didn't display too much enthusiasm for the book. That is, until he read it—as well as various other books from Strieber, including the truly chilling 1984 book, *Warday*, which is a hair-raising tale of a disastrous, limited nuclear exchange between the United States and the former Soviet Union. Conroy was now interested; *very* interested. Conroy was clearly destined to dig further, which he did. That Strieber was from San Antonio and Conroy worked there made things easier, too.

Conroy did an extensive interview with Strieber in April 1987, followed by a face-to-face meeting three months later. Conroy was initially planning to write an article or several on Strieber. He quickly realized, though, that there was enough material for a book—a book that would address the many and various intricacies from a detached, open-minded perspective. Conroy was destined not to remain detached, though, and particularly so when he too was caught up in a definitive maelstrom of mystery and conspiracy.

The Intimidation Continues

On one occasion, at the height of his research into Strieber's story, Conroy encountered in his very own bedroom what he described as "a kind of shadow man, completely black, poised in the classic pose of Rodin's 'The Thinker.'" This sounds very much like what today are known as the Shadow People—malevolent, supernatural entities that have clear and undeniable links to the equally sinister Men in Black, who, as we have seen, have nothing to do with the government (despite what the phenomenally successful *Men in Black* movies might say . . .) and everything to do with the UFO phenomenon itself. Strange noises plagued Conroy, waking him from a dead sleep almost in a manipulative, playful fashion, but which bordered on the unsettling. Then, there was the matter of those infamous 'copters.

It was one particular morning in March 1987 that Ed Conroy found himself a target of whoever it is that flies the mysterious helicopters.

It appeared to be a Bell 47, said Conroy, and it lacked any identifying markings, which is very curious, but absolutely typical of the helicopters of the phantom type. Notably, said Conroy, "What was remarkable about this particular helicopter was the inordinate amount of attention it seemed to be paying to my building." In no time, and shortly after the Bell 47 finally exited the area, a totally black helicopter was on the scene. Follow-up visits occurred—something which prompted Conroy to contact the Federal Aviation Administration for answers. No luck there.

Things got even more intense in 1988 when Conroy was practically seeing helicopters here, there, and everywhere. And particularly, again, in the direct vicinity of his apartment, including the huge, double-rotor, military Chinooks. Conroy even saw some of the helicopters vanish—as in *literally* vanish. Some kind of stealthy cloaking technology, perhaps?

Then, in June 1988, something else happened: while Conroy was out of town, someone changed the message on his answering machine, in his apartment. And it was changed again. And again. Clearly, someone was screwing with Conroy—perhaps even trying to plunge him into states of paranoia and fear. On top of that, Conroy started to hear strange clicking noises on his phone. Weird, unintelligible voices would call, saturated in electric static and which echoed the tactics of the Men in Black when, in the 1960s, John Keel was investigating the infamous wave of Mothman sightings in Point Pleasant, West Virginia.

And Finally, an Area 51 Connection

You will recall that one of Strieber's most intriguing revelations from his experiences was that the visitors had a deep awareness of the nature of the human soul to the extent that they had the ability to manipulate it, even to recycle it into the body of a newly born child. It just so happens that back in 1989, a man named Bob Lazar claimed that in the latter part of 1988 he'd spent several months working out at a subsection of Area 51 called S-4. Much of Lazar's story is beyond the scope of this book, but it's worth noting that according to Lazar, while at S-4 he read highly classified files which stated the aliens viewed us as "containers." But containers of what? According to Lazar, when pressed by Las Vegas, Nevada–based news journalist George Knapp in 1989, possibly containers of souls. Remember too that Strieber had made a connection between Rotron and Area 51— and it was someone within Rotron who was determined to torture Strieber with late-night phone calls in 1992.

We might well ask, does the government know something about the soul-recycling angle of the alien abduction phenomenon. Is it something that the government—and/or the military and intelligence communities— prefers us not to know? Could there be something ominous and disturbing about the whole soul-stealing angle? One person who has addressed this area very deeply is Nigel Kerner. He has written two books on the alien abduction–human soul angle: *The Song of the Greys* and *Grey Aliens and the Harvesting of Souls*.

Secrets of the Soul

Danielle Silverman—Nigel Kerner's assistant—prepared the following for me:

[Kerner] went on to delineate a fascinating concept, explaining that a "soul" might be a derivational information field that comes out of a natural cadence that came into the Universe with the big bang. This field holds the power to maintain information in what he called a morphogenetic electro-spatial field with an eternal scope of existence in whatever form circumstance allows. The soul is thus an ancestrally contiguous and coherent mechanism for holding information.

Nigel argued that if the Greys are an artificially created and manufactured roboidal form then they would find our facility for "soul" an analogue of their own creators. This would be an analogue that they would want to try to combine with their own natures themselves. The "Greys" he argued were synthetic biological programmed artificially intelligent machine entities sent out as super intelligent robots far more advanced than those we now ourselves send out to explore the Universe.

They are, however, subject to wear and tear as indeed are all atomically derived entities through the second law of thermodynamics which drives them into greater and greater states of decay with time. A non-atomic property however, such as "soul," is immune to the second law. Thus this property was their ultimate goal, their "holy grail" so to speak. It was a property that they could never know or understand in its own terms as purely atomic artificial creations. Their only perception of it was the effect it has on atoms, the difference in other words between a naturally living entity and their artificial state.

Ironically, what these artificially intelligent entities are seeking is eternal survivability. The Greys and any physical life that they might reconstitute from the DNA codes they carry on behalf of their creators, cannot access the state beyond death. They have no "soul" they cannot be born. They are trying to use us as a bridge into "soul" writing their programs into us through genetic engineering and implantation so that through us they can tap into an eternal existence.

If the thoughts, theories, and conclusions of Nigel Kerner are correct, then it's no wonder the government would open files on, and place under surveillance, Whitley Strieber and Ed Conroy. Telling the world that the primary goal of alien abductions is to reap the human soul as a means to ensure immortality for the Greys would almost certainly be one of the very last things the government would ever want to do. Indeed, how could one reveal such an immense secret to the world without it causing widespread fear and chaos? The likely answer is: one couldn't. If Strieber *was* getting close to the truth with his comments concerning aliens and human souls, then it makes great sense that officialdom would place him under a state of deep surveillance. And Conroy too, given that at the time all of his weirdness went down he was working on a book on Strieber.

The truth of the Greys, alien abductions, and our souls might not be out there (to slightly warp a famous phrase from *The X-Files*): it might be buried in the classified, deep-underground vaults of Area 51.

17 A WITNESS TO AN UNDERGROUND REALM SPEAKS

Christa Tilton is someone who has been a fixture in the alien abduction field for several decades, and who today keeps a low profile. It's notable that many of Tilton's personal experiences eerily mirror those of Myrna Hansen and Judy Doraty. Her experiences also demonstrate that she was watched secretly and quietly, and subjected to experiences reported by victims of the MILAB phenomenon. For Tilton, it all began in the summer of 1987, specifically the month of July. It was one particular night that Tilton experienced a period of missing time which ran into an undetermined number of hours. It was only thanks to extensive hypnotic regression that Tilton was able to unveil the erased experiences.

It all began, as so many such events do, at home. Late on the night in question, Tilton suddenly found herself feeling odd, spaced out, weird—descriptions which are acutely familiar in abduction history. Like so many abductees, Tilton did not go quietly or willingly: she was dragged out of her bed unceremoniously and taken to a craft. The next thing Tilton recalled was being inside some sort of vehicle; a UFO, she suspected. A figure who stood by her motioned her to take a drink from a glass, and it had the almost instant effect of wiping out the lethargy and drugged-out feeling she'd had when she first woke up. Whatever it was, it was a definitive stimulant.

When fully recovered, Tilton was guided out of the craft by the same character—at which point she could now see she was on a hill shrouded in darkness, somewhere in the countryside. But where, exactly, she had no idea. As her eyes acclimated to the dark, however, she could see what looked like the entrance to a cave or cavern. Suddenly, what was clearly another figure appeared on the scene. He was wearing a red suit like that of a fighter pilot, and he carried an automatic weapon. The "Man in Red" greeted them.

Then all three proceeded to the cavernous abode.

Going Underground

As Tilton got closer, she could see a dim light in the depths of what was clearly a long tunnel. They were soon met by a second guard who was also in a red jumpsuit. They approached what Tilton assumed was a checkpoint, as there were cameras strategically placed on the walls. Tilton was then directed to a small vehicle that took her to another section of the cavernous facility which, she suspected, was a carved-out section of a massive mountain. The Dulce base, perhaps? It's not at all an impossibility.

After what was a short journey further into the subterranean world, they exited the vehicle and Tilton was told to stand on something that resembled a pair of scales. A computer screen flickered, and she was soon presented with a card that she deduced was some kind of ID. By this time, Tilton was not just puzzled, but scared. She wanted to know where she was and why. And what was coming next. The man in the red outfit, says Tilton, made an enigmatic statement that intrigued her, but which didn't really provide any answers, as she notes: "I asked my guide where we were going and why. He didn't say too much the whole time except that he was to show me some things that I need to know for future reference." Precisely what was meant by "future reference" was not made clear.

From there, Tilton was taken to a massive elevator. Noticing that she was staring at the elevator door, the man said that they were presently on the first floor but were about to descend to the second floor. Oddly, the elevator didn't have doors: it was like an old-style dumbwaiter, but one big enough to hold people. On the second floor, the personnel were dressed in outfits of a different color. Tilton was then motioned to a long hallway, which she and the others walked along. Offices filled both side of the hallway, many of them containing vast arrays of computer banks. The lighting was odd: everywhere was lit up, but Tilton could not see any sources for the light. There were no lights, lamps, bulbs, nothing. It was as she was staring around the tunnel that she came face-to-face with a group of small, black-eyed aliens. To say that Tilton was stunned and shocked to the core would be a mammoth understatement.

The aliens were bustling around a group of small, UFO-like craft— perhaps engaged in repairing them, Tilton thought. She was quickly taken from the area and then directed to another elevator, which took her to even lower levels of the facility, specifically level five. On exiting the elevator, Tilton felt a sudden and inexplicable sense of cold fear. There was something very wrong about this particular level. Tilton's instincts were right on target.

As if aware too that level five was filled with danger, her guide—the man in red, again—told her to stay close to him: that way she would be safe. She couldn't help but see that several of the guards on this floor were staring at her, but in a harsh, almost sinister, fashion. Tilton wanted out. Fast. But there was more to come before she would finally be able to leave.

A Room Filled with Fear

Tilton was then taken to a room where she was told to change clothes— into what was somewhat like a hospital gown. Once again, she was told to stand on a pair of scales. As she did so, a screen near her lit up and penetrating frequencies rattled her eardrums. Tilton was then directed to head out of the room and into a long corridor, much like the one on the higher floor. Cameras were everywhere. And the whole area smelled of formaldehyde. That was not good.

A large room was soon in sight, and Tilton was compelled to look inside—encouraged to, even. She recalls: "I saw these huge large tanks with computerized gauges hooked to them and a huge arm-like device that extended from the top of some tubing down into the tanks. The tanks were about 4 feet tall so standing where I was I could not see inside them."

Tilton also remembers that something was being stirred in the tanks, but she was not told what, precisely. The guide then forcibly grabbed Tilton, roughly tugging her along the tunnel. She soon found herself in what was a huge laboratory. Grey aliens were working alongside people. Machines whirred, equipment flashed and buzzed. It was like sci-fi, but this was sci-*fact*.

Fear overwhelmed Tilton when she was ordered, by one of the staff, to sit on a table in the middle of the room, with one of the eerie Greys staring at her. The man looked grimmer than grim. Tilton refused, at which point the man said things would go easy if she went along with his orders. Tilton knew a veiled threat when she heard one, so she did as she was told.

Then another man wearing a lab coat entered the room, and the two men shook hands. Suddenly, the temperature in the room dropped drastically and Tilton started to shake. Her guide smiled, said that all would be okay, and left the room. A second Grey then entered the room and Tilton suddenly felt weak, drowsy, and disoriented. She realized she was now horizontal and being examined internally. An intense pain caused Tilton to scream, at which point one of the doctors applied a cold substance to her stomach, which alleviated the pain. In quick time, the procedure— whatever it may have been—was over. Tilton was then told to go to a smaller room nearby, where she dressed.

By this time, Tilton was far angrier than scared, and she screamed that this was wrong, that it should not be allowed. It fell on deaf ears. She was simply told that it was all "necessary" and that she should try to forget the whole experience. Her guide was slightly more talkative at this point and told Tilton that she was in a very "sensitive place" and that she would likely return in a few years' time. But for the safety of her very life, Tilton could not be told where exactly she was.

With that, they made their way to one of the small transit vehicles that seemed to be everywhere and made a brief drive to what turned out to be an exit. On the final leg, says Tilton, she was exposed to the horrific sight of a group of people—men and women—in canisters. They were immobile, like shop-window mannequins. But these were no dummies. Other containers housed various kinds of animals—all of which led Tilton to believe that some deeply sinister operation was afoot, an operation that involved human scientists, the military, and alien entities. Then Tilton was taken to the elevator she had originally descended in, and directed to the craft that she originally arrived in. The next thing she remembered was being back home, unaware of how she got there.

18 SURVEILLANCE IN THE 1990s

G reg Bishop is a longtime observer of the UFO phenomenon and a good friend of mine. He's also a respected researcher and author who has covered numerous aspects of the UFO subject, including the contactee phenomenon of the 1950s, cattle mutilations, and the Roswell affair of July 1947. Bishop is someone who also found himself the subject of secret surveillance—and possibly a secret file—when he began to liaise with certain people in ufology who had dug into the matter of what the US government, military, and intelligence community know about the phenomenon of alien abductions.

In part, at least, this was very likely as a result of the publication of his 2005 book, *Project Beta*, which was focused on the bizarre and troubling saga of Paul Bennewitz, Judy Doraty, and Myrna Hansen. All three, you will recall, had significant links to the alien abduction issue and the government's knowledge of what's going on. I say "in part" because there is strong evidence that Bishop was being watched much earlier than that.

Someone Intercepts the Mail

In 1994, Bishop conducted an extensive interview with abductee Dr. Karla Turner for his now defunct magazine, *The Excluded Middle*, which was run by Bishop and two friends: Robert Larson and Peter Stenshoel. It was a comprehensive, ten-page Q&A which got right to the heart of Turner's experiences. It was not without its oddities, however.

The interview was undertaken at the home of a friend of Bishop's named Wes Nations. The night before, Bishop work up in the early hours at 1:11, 2:22, 3:33, and 4:44. When Bishop mentioned this to Turner, she commented that this was commonplace when it came to alien abductees. On top of that, Nations told Bishop that shortly after he had left to head back home, a number of people in "khaki outfits" were seen roaming around Nations' home, and soon a fire broke out on his property. Bishop said that the fire did not do any appreciable damage, but added that it "made all of us wonder just what it was that Karla Turner uncovered." Indeed.

Bishop and Turner developed a good rapport and respect for each other—to the extent that they stayed in touch and became good friends. But as the friendship developed, and as Turner and Bishop spent more and more time digging into her experiences, something very strange and sinister happened: *someone started to take notice.* They did so in an undeniably chilling fashion.

Back in the early to mid-1990s, the internet was hardly up and running in the fashion it is today, so the pair corresponded by mail. This resulted in something very strange, as Bishop himself notes: "Mail tampering is the darling of clinical paranoids; but nearly every piece of mail that the late researcher/abductee sent to my PO Box looked like it had been tampered with or opened. Since this is easy to do without having to be obvious, we figured someone was interested in her work enough to make it clear that she was being monitored. She took to putting a piece of transparent tape over the flap and writing 'sealed' on it. Karla pretty much took it for granted after a while, and suggested I do likewise."

But that was not the only example of high strangeness tinged with a degree of concern and paranoia that hit Bishop.

Freaky Photographers on the Loose

During roughly the same time Bishop and Turner were experiencing mail tampering on a large scale—and specifically in relation to Turner's alien abduction experiences—Bishop came to believe that his phone was being monitored. It probably was: as Bishop has revealed, over the course of several months he found himself hit by *more than ten mysterious phone calls per day*. No one ever spoke when Bishop answered those particular calls. Instead, there was nothing but clicking and humming. Bishop was so concerned about the strange noises, for a while he even worried that "the sounds were designed to control my thoughts in some way and [I] always hung up quickly." Matters only came to a halt when Bishop got himself an answering machine.

One day, in this very same period, Bishop happened to look out the window of his living room and saw a man sitting in a car directly opposite his house and looking in Bishop's direction. As if realizing that he had been seen, the man brazenly got out of his car, raised a camera, took a photo of Bishop's home, got back into the car, and drove off. John Keel—who had experienced this very same phenomenon in the 1960s while pursuing tales of Mothman and the Men in Black in Point Pleasant, West Virginia— called such characters "phantom photographers."

An Insider or a Disinformer?

If that was not enough, at the same time Bishop suspected his phone was being monitored, he was also approached—quite out of the blue—by a man named Mike Younger. At least, that was the name he gave Bishop. One can never be entirely sure of anything in this mind-bending game— and that most certainly includes names. Younger reportedly had a very good reason for seeking out Bishop. Bishop recalls that Younger claimed to have "looked at my file," something which Bishop said both shocked and flattered him. It got Bishop's keen attention, too—which was almost certainly Younger's primary goal.

Bishop recalls, "Other things I was told started to bother me. Mike said that someone sitting outside or in another building could see what was on my computer screen by scanning the signal of the CRT [Cathode-Ray Tube]." As we'll see soon, there may well have been something to that particularly controversial claim. But who exactly was this mysterious figure, an enigmatic character who claimed to have just about all the skinny on both UFOs and Bishop himself?

According to Younger, he worked with an arm of US naval intelligence—out at Area 51, no less. Younger and Bishop typically met in cafés and restaurants, during which Younger showed Bishop countless pages of material on all manner of issues relative to UFOs. Younger also claimed that he and a number of his colleagues were working hard to try to reveal the truth about the UFO phenomenon to the public. We're talking about what, today, is known as UFO disclosure.

Younger eventually cut off contact with Bishop and vanished into the shadows, as government spooks are so adeptly prone to doing. Bishop was told, years later, that Younger died of a heart attack at the very early age of thirty. True or not, Bishop was uneasy about the whole thing. And, he remained uneasy for a long time. Now, we will return to Bishop's computer, which, Mike Younger claimed, was under constant surveillance by whoever it was that had such a deep interest in Bishop and his activities—some relative to alien abduction issues.

The Spying Continues and a Death Looms on the Horizon

Jim Keith was a researcher-author who focused on conspiracy theories—ufological and political. One of the things that particularly intrigued Keith was the very weird phenomenon of the black helicopters, craft which just so happen to play an integral role in monitoring alien abductees, as we have seen. Keith wrote two books on this particular subject, such was the wealth of material he had carefully and scrupulously accumulated on the controversy, *Black Helicopters Over America: Strikeforce for the New World Order* in 1994, and 1997's *Black Helicopters II: The Endgame Strategy*.

From August 31 to September 3, 1999, Bishop and Keith corresponded via email on a disturbing issue that, at the time, was affecting both of them: computer problems. Very suspicious problems. On the thirty-first, Keith wrote to Bishop: "Interesting things happening with my computer. Last week I was hit with a virus, and all my personal files were wiped out. Don't know whether to chalk this up to a conspiracy, but I know a couple of other writers in this field who had the same thing happen to them at about the same time."

On the following day, Bishop replied, informing Keith that all of his articles had been trashed, and deliberately deleted from the trash folder too. Keith responded by saying he was now working on a new article on "the number of investigative reporters and editors being hacked."

Then, on September 3, Bishop wrote to Keith: "There are a few possibilities: I was hacked through the modem, I was given a virus that only affects my article folder and no other Word files, or someone broke in the house and deleted them. I guess I'll believe the story that makes me feel best."

Keith's final email to Bishop, of September 3, read: "Thanks for the statement, Greg. So far I've turned up nine political conspiracy sites that were hacked in the same time period."

And why was it Keith's final email to Bishop? Because on September 7, Keith was no more. *He was stone-cold dead.*

Accident or Murder?

Jim Keith had headed out to the annual Burning Man festival in the Nevada desert, a day before the event began. While on stage, Keith lost his balance and fell to the ground. At first, Keith thought he had just badly bruised his leg. By the morning, he was in such agony he had to call for paramedics, who quickly took him to Washoe Medical Center in Reno.

Keith was told he had fractured his tibia and that he was to be prepped for surgery—which would require him to be anaesthetized. This was when things got really weird.

Keith put a call through to a friend in the conspiracy field—George Pickard—and told him that one of the attendants at the hospital had the same name as someone he had debated on the matter of the black helicopters, and just a few months earlier. Coincidence? Who knows. As the time for surgery got closer, Keith got more and more anxious. He said to his nephew, Chris Davis, "I have a feeling that if they put me under I'm not coming back. I know if I get put under, I am going to die."

That's *exactly* what happened: a blood clot took Keith's life. The field of conspiracy theorizing was both stunned and suspicious by this very untimely and tragic state of affairs. An unfortunate event, or a well-orchestrated murder by culprits unknown? That was the question asked most frequently in the immediate wake of Keith's death. It's a question that still gets asked today. The final word on this specific issue goes to Greg Bishop: "I would prefer to think that there was no connection to the weird computer problems."

That's not all, though. Bishop admits the following:

While working on Project Beta [which was between 2003 and 2005] I had the chance to talk to a few former intelligence and military people, whom I found fascinating and not a little intimidating at times. They played the intelligence game with me, sometimes using me as a go-between for information that might answer some of their old questions about many subjects. I often knew that this was going on, but probably not always. . . . As a result, I became interested in the intelligence game, how to play it, and what happens to those who do. They always hold the cards, and to get anything, you have to play the game.

Bishop still occasionally plays the game, but fortunately—and to his credit—he has left the world of paranoia and fear far behind him.

19 MILABS IN THE TWENTY-FIRST CENTURY

As we have seen, so-called MILABS—military abductions—date back to 1957 with the saga of Antonio Villas Boas, a Brazilian man whose encounter with aliens may actually not have been anything of the sort. Very much the same can be said for the 1973 experiences of Calvin Parker and Charles Hickson. Now, to demonstrate that the phenomenon of MILAB is still very much ongoing, we'll take a look at a significant case from 2015. It comes from my own files and tells the story of Charlie from Shreveport, Louisiana.

Charlie contacted me in late 2016, after seeing me talking about extraterrestrial abductions on the History Channel's hugely popular show *Ancient Aliens*. It was on January 2, 2015, that Charlie had an encounter that he wishes he could forever forget. Unfortunately, that seems unlikely. The event in question is embedded in his mind and, in all likelihood, will remain there. As Charlie told me, when we met at the annual Texas Bigfoot Conference in Jefferson, Texas, in October 2016, he has conscious recall of the abduction, which occurred when he was nineteen years of age.

A Screen Memory and Parallels with *The Matrix*

At the time, Charlie was living at home, which was a small house in a quiet, isolated area on the fringes of the city. His parents were out of town at the time, visiting old friends in Florida for a post–Christmas Day celebration. Charlie was stretched out on the couch, watching TV—about two in the morning—when he suddenly had a weird compulsion to go to the living room window. He cautiously opened the blinds slightly, to see a police car parked right outside the house. He stared at it for a few moments, debating whether or not he should go outside and ask the police if all was okay, which is exactly what he finally did. But this was no normal encounter with the police.

Charlie explained that as he walked down the drive, he started to feel antsy and worried—but he didn't really know why. It wasn't just the presence of the police vehicle; it was almost as if he was "half-awake," as Charlie worded it, and as if he was in a bizarre dream-like world. He likened it to the theme of the 1999 Keanu Reeves movie *The Matrix*, in which the human race is unknowingly living in a virtual reality world created by hostile, advanced machines.

As Charlie cautiously approached the car, he could see that the driver was staring intently at him, and as if he knew in advance that Charlie would come outside and walk to the car. What really frightened Charlie, though, was the look on the face of the police officer: he had what Charlie called "a really weird smile." I asked Charlie what he meant by that, and he said that it was "an insane smile; like crazy and dangerous." Even stranger, the man's partner was also staring intently at Charlie, and with an equally unsettling grin, too. Then, things became a blur. The car and the two officers vanished. In their place was an egg-shaped object the size of a large truck.

A Terror-Filled Abduction Begins

Charlie tried to run back to the safety of the house. No luck. He felt like he was running in slow motion—and getting slower by the step. The next thing Charlie recalled was standing in a field that backed onto woods behind the family's home. The two men were standing before him, but this time they didn't look like police officers. Rather, they were classic Men in Black: they had the dark suits, old-style fedora hats, and pale skin and enlarged eyes. They weren't locals, to say the least.

The pair of MIB grabbed Charlie and hauled him aboard the craft which was hovering about three feet off the ground. In what seemed like only seconds, but which he felt, later, had to have been longer, Charlie found himself dressed in an outfit that reminded him of "a surgeon's scrubs." And he was lying horizontal on a long, thin bed. Terror kicked in when Charlie found himself unable to move: his wrists, arms, and ankles were shackled to the bed. His heart thumped wildly. Even more so when he saw three small figures walk into the room and stand next to the bed—two on the left side and one on the right. They were all around four-and-a-half to five feet in height, with large, hairless heads and huge black eyes.

A Vision of Disaster

One of the creatures touched Charlie on his right shoulder, something that instantly created an image in his mind of the Earth coming to an end: the planet was in ruins, entire nations were destroyed, billions were dead, thick clouds completely blocked out the sun, and gigantic radioactive mushroom clouds dominated just about everywhere. It was clear that World War Three had begun. It had ended, too. And the human race was also at its end.

Suddenly, the horrific, cataclysmic vision was gone. Worse was to come, though. Charlie could feel something cold and metallic in his nostril, "like a probe." He felt his fingers clench, and his toes, too. Then a popping sound in his head, which led to another graphic vision. This one was very different, though. It was of the Earth, but thousands of years after nuclear Armageddon. The world was finally repairing itself. What was left of our great cities was swamped by massive vegetation, trees, bushes, vines, and moss. Nature was reclaiming the planet. Not one person was in sight. There was, however, an abundance of wildlife. Animals were everywhere, playing, eating, sleeping, and roaming around. The implication—as Charlie saw it—was that the aliens were telling him that we, the human race, "had our chance and screwed it all up." So it was time for other life forms to hold the position of the number one species on the planet. In our place were the animals we kept as pets, for food, and as entertainment in zoos and circuses—and, of course, countless numbers of wild animals. We were nothing but memories, maybe not even that.

Interestingly, Charlie told me that he felt a world without people was not a bad thing at all. For the human race, yes, of course it was a tragedy. But for the rest of just about every other living thing on the planet, it was a relief.

The Abduction Comes to an End

Charlie's mind then swung right back to that sterile room; the three alien entities were still standing around him. He suddenly realized that the device in his nose was gone. He suggested to me that perhaps that same device had the ability to insert images into a person's mind. On that same track, Charlie suggested that perhaps what he'd seen were not literal views of the future. He had pondered the idea that maybe what he had seen was something like a highly sophisticated virtual reality game—a game designed to warn him of what *could* happen, rather than something that was *definitely* going to occur.

Moments later, Charlie found himself in the front yard of the family home—with no idea how he'd gotten there. At the edge of the drive was that same police car, and the same officers too. Both were leaning toward him, still wearing those disturbing smiles. The car then slowly drove away in complete silence and vanished into the darkness of the early morning. Charlie stared into that same darkness for a few minutes, then shakily made his way to bed. He woke up the next morning feeling feverish, cold, and exhausted. A visit to his doctor revealed a severe chest infection, which took several weeks to clear up.

When I spoke with Charlie, he admitted to me that after the encounter he started to read a great deal of books on the subject of alien abductions, and had come to believe that the police car and the two officers amounted to nothing less than a false memory created by the aliens. He suspected that perhaps the vehicle was really a UFO and that his mind was "made to remember seeing a car." There was one other thing that Charlie wanted to share with me—and get my opinion on, too. It all revolved around another abduction. But this one was not a kidnapping by aliens, but by what Charlie was sure was some clandestine arm of the US military.

High Strangeness Begins

Charlie found it intriguing—and so did I—that the follow-up incident occurred when his parents were again out of town, just a month or so later. He admitted that he felt more than a bit concerned. This does make sense: as on the previous occasion, he was all alone and on a piece of property that was very isolated. And when the sun set, the area was overwhelmed by the darkness of winter. It was the perfect location from which to take someone and have no one else have any inkling of what had happened. Now, there was a possibility that the same thing was going to happen again. The day began normally. Charlie did a bunch of chores and then met a friend in the afternoon, at a restaurant. By the time he got home it was around six and he was ready to watch a couple movies he had recorded.

At about nine, the phone rang. The caller ID displayed two words: "Private Caller." Charlie chose to let it go to answering machine. As the recorded voice of his father kicked in, the person at the other end of the line abruptly hung up. The same thing happened about twenty minutes later, and about an hour after that. After the fourth time, Charlie answered the phone, shouting, "Who the fuck is this?" Again, the line went dead. Charlie went to the living room window. No one was there. Thankfully, there was no police car, either. Whether it was due to nerves or something else, Charlie had a strange dizzy spell that forced him to lie down on the couch. The odd feeling soon went away. Charlie didn't know it, but the worst was yet to come.

Abductors Who Weren't Aliens

Charlie told me that at some point he fell asleep on the couch, and was woken up—at what time, he wasn't sure—by a man in a black military-style outfit, whose gloved hand was firmly over his mouth. The man, a thirty-something with a southern accent, warned him not to say a word. As Charlie frantically tried to fight back, two other men—both dressed the same—sprung out of the shadows, ensuring that Charlie had no chance of getting away. As the three held Charlie, and as one told him to quit trying to fight them, another man in fatigues came out of the kitchen and quickly injected something into Charlie's arm. The next thing he remembered was waking up in the back of a large van, surrounded by the four men who had somehow stealthily invaded his home. Or at least he assumed they were the same men: everything was, unsurprisingly, a blur. He found himself sitting in a chair, as were the four men. The van and the seats had clearly been converted, said Charlie, to allow for some sort of interrogation to proceed—which is exactly what happened. A needle was inserted into Charlie's upper left arm and he was injected with something that calmed him down significantly—and very quickly, too.

While the men were not overly threatening, they were certainly forceful when it came to telling Charlie that they required him to answer all of their questions and, afterward, to say nothing to anyone. He didn't, until he came up to my book table at the Bigfoot gig, which was more than a year later. They wanted answers to more than a few questions:

- How long had he been interested in the UFO subject? Charlie replied, truthfully, that he had no interest prior to the very strange encounter of January 2, 2015.

- Had he ever had any dreams about extraterrestrials and UFOs? No.

- Was he vegetarian? No, Charlie was not. But he admitted to having urges to stop eating meat, which had begun just a few weeks before.

Then the situation became more intriguing—and, for Charlie, disturbing too.

Questions about Armageddon

One of the men leaned forward and told Charlie that they knew all about his encounter of the very close type, which had occurred just after the new year, and said they wanted him to share with them every aspect of the incident that he could remember. He said his mouth was dry and he asked for something to drink. He was given a bottle of water from a blue cooler in the corner of the van. After knocking back most of the water, Charlie told the men what he had seen—while one of them recorded his words on a handheld device. He shared with them the issue of the police car which he suspected was not really a police car after all. And he described how the two supposed police officers morphed into a pair of MIB, something which seemed to catch the particular attention of the men, since they asked Charlie to describe their appearance and their clothing.

Charlie's description of a vision of worldwide nuclear war provoked the one man who asked more questions than the others to ask if he, Charlie, had any firm ideas as to which cities were destroyed. Charlie admitted that he had no idea, but he said that the images in his head led him to believe that the war was global: no one was free of the destruction. And he added, that the sky was thick with dark clouds as far as the eye could see was a good indication of the scale of the event. The same man asked, in words broadly as follows, "So this was not a limited strike?" Charlie replied that no, it was not. He went on to share the vision he had of a future Earth which was empty of people, and how the animals had reclaimed the world for themselves. Then, Charlie made a big mistake—although he wouldn't realize that until it was too late.

The MILABS Team Expresses Concerns about Alien Implants

After sharing the story of the world of the future and a devastating Third World War, Charlie mentioned the issue of the aliens inserting something in one of his nostrils. For a moment, there was silence, after which the main man told Charlie to listen to him. And to listen to him very carefully. In what was clearly a rare example of frankness and openness in the world of MILABS, the man explained to Charlie that we have in our midst a dangerous race of extraterrestrials who are routinely implanting devices into large numbers of the American population—devices that have the ability to control and manipulate people as they see fit. Very controversially, Charlie claimed the man told him that certain mass shootings were the work of implanted individuals who were enslaved by the aliens.

The number of implanted people was growing by the day, Charlie was told, and we, the human race, are losing the battle at a shockingly fast pace. He also told Charlie that the primary insertion point for the implants was the nose. Charlie was then informed that they would need to "scan" him, to see if he too had been implanted. One of the other men leaned forward and casually waved a small device, "like a hairdryer," over Charlie's face and head, after which the man said something like, "It's okay; he's clean." Looking back on things, Charlie suspected the man had performed the same task on numerous other occasions, which is why he was almost blasé about the whole thing.

The team then confided in Charlie that not only was the nostril the entrance point for the implantation, but it was also through the nostril that the aliens could temporarily insert devices that would provoke graphic imagery into the minds of the targeted individuals. To everyone's relief, Charlie fell into the second category, rather than the far more ominous first group.

Notably, the man added that the implantation issue was being viewed by those in the know as a threat equally as great as that posed by the likes of rogue nations seeking to gain or create nuclear weapons.

The Experience Ends

With all that now done, Charlie was driven back to his home—and actually given an apology for the rough handling several hours earlier. Notably, Charlie realized that the drive from where the questioning took place to his home only took about fifteen or twenty minutes, revealing to him that after he had been taken by the men, they had parked fairly close by. He also recalled that for the first five or six minutes, the drive back was extremely bumpy. This led Charlie to suspect that the van was on a dirt road, maybe one which ran through nearby woods. Maybe, said Charlie, it was in the woods where the interrogation occurred. It made sense. On arriving back at his home, a door was opened, Charlie got out, one of the men nodded at him, the door was closed, and the van was quickly gone.

It's not surprising that Charlie didn't get any sleep that night, as his mind—in a fair degree of turmoil—kept him wide awake. Of course, there is the fairly significant, and curious, fact that the MILABS team felt the need to share so much highly classified data with Charlie. Was this a means to get the word out, subtly, as to what was going on under our noses, and literally so? After all, Charlie *didn't* stay quiet: he told me, and now I'm sharing it with you, an untold number of people. So maybe there *was* a plan to share the facts with Charlie, knowing that he probably wouldn't keep his mouth shut. The good cop/bad cop routine may well have been skillfully orchestrated to see not only how Charlie would respond, but even those now reading this very book, as well as many others focused on the alien abduction controversy.

Charlie also said to me that he felt a high degree of sympathy for the men who abducted him—"It must be a tough thing to hide," he said—which made me suspect that he was affected by a small degree of Stockholm syndrome, a condition which makes the captured develop an affinity with their captor.

The idea that hordes of hostile aliens could be secretly implanting who knows how many people does, admittedly, sound like wild sci-fi. But as we'll see in the next chapter, the human race is coming perilously close to doing exactly the same.

20 THE IMPLANT ISSUE

There is absolutely no doubt that certain elements of the US government, and particularly the Air Force, have taken a deep interest in the stories of alien abductees being implanted with strange, small objects—the purpose of which both baffles and disturbs those tasked with monitoring the situation. As we have seen, the military's involvement in this area dates back to at least 1980, when implanted abductee Myrna Hansen was examined at New Mexico–based Lovelace Medical Center. While all this might sound like something straight out of a wild science-fiction movie—aliens taking over people's minds and controlling them with tiny devices—the fact is that such technology is all too real. There is a very good reason why the alien implant issue should be taken seriously: we, the human race, are now creating our very own equivalents of the technology that aliens may have had for who knows how many years. Maybe, for millennia. In other words, this technology is all too real.

Disturbingly, there are people who are pushing for us all to be implanted with devices designed to track our movements, record our medical histories, and provide information on our social-media activity. One of these people is science fiction writer Elizabeth Moon. She is no fool: she has degrees from the University of Texas and Rice University. In 2012, Moon made a statement that sent shivers up the spines of many—and was reported on by the BBC: "I would insist on every individual having a unique ID permanently attached—a barcode if you will—an implanted chip to provide an easy, fast inexpensive way to identify individuals."

It's hardly surprising that Rice's words provoked a great deal of commentary and observation. Despite her earnest belief that we should all be tagged like animals, Rice is wrong. Dead wrong.

The Rise of the Chips

The day we become a microchipped species is the day freedom is gone—forever. Of course, some might argue that there are some advantages to being chipped, provided that the chip is used in a benevolent fashion. For example, the chipping of cats and dogs has reunited families with their beloved pets on probably thousands of occasions. One could also make a case that chipping children in similar fashion would help to quickly bring kidnappings to a sudden halt—or even deter people from abducting victims in the first place. That would all be fine if the chips planned for us were solely designed to help locate people. But when a chip contains just about all of our private material—and all because the government deems it necessary—things are going just way too far.

The problem, today, is that all too many people would likely sign up to be chipped. Maybe even in droves. Why? Because the fear factor would be rolled out. Get your chip or fall victim to the terrorist and the gun-waving madman. Or things might become even more draconian and Orwellian than that: either get chipped or consider yourself a subversive, a person of interest, a threat to national security. You think it couldn't happen? We're already on the way to that nightmarish world.

Fortunately, the mainstream media has waded into this affair, including the *New York Daily News*, which said, "The proposal isn't too far-fetched—it is already technically possible to 'barcode' a human—but does it violate our rights to privacy?" Of course it violates our rights to privacy. Only a fool—or someone pushing for widespread chipping—would ever suggest otherwise.

The American Civil Liberties Union (ACLU) has also taken careful notice of this growing threat—and threat is without doubt the perfect way to describe it. The ACLU says: "To have a record of everywhere you go and everything you do would be a frightening thing. Once we let the government and businesses go down the road of nosing around in our lives, we're going to quickly lose all our privacy."

Then there's this point made by the *Inquirer*: "There is also the fear that this technology could be used by unscrupulous people or criminals, by competing corporations, or even by some agencies in the government, for illegal information gathering or surveillance, or for some immoral objectives." They make a very good point: Let's say that your personal microchip contains your smartphone number, your Social Security number, your Facebook password, your email password, and personal data on your health. If such data was stolen by hackers—literally hacking into your chip—then who knows the level of chaos that might ensue. And if that hacker is just one of tens of thousands who work for a government body—such as the ever-eavesdropping NSA—it would not take long at all before the world's biggest database came to fruition. And in a terrible fashion—one that would have George Orwell spinning in his grave.

Wittingly Implanted

While the issue of government-issued implants has been discussed for years, and chiefly from a theoretical perspective, few are aware that some American families are already implanted. We're not talking about something akin to alien abductions, where the implant is placed in the body of the victim against their will and, in some cases, even without their knowledge. We're talking about complete and utter fools who actually signed up to be implanted. Leading the pack in the beyond-foolish stakes was the Jacobs family of Florida: Jeffrey, Leslie, and their son, Derek. In May of 2002, the whole family was implanted with small devices containing their medical histories.

Again, if used in the right way, such technology does have its advantages:

if a person collapses on the street and a scan of their chip shows they have diabetes, such a revelation might very well help to stabilize that person in quick time. The same goes for conditions like epilepsy and heart-related issues. But who's to say that our medical data wouldn't be used against us? Couldn't happen? It certainly could. Imagine if your chip showed that your cholesterol levels are extremely high: an insurance company might be very reluctant to offer you coverage.

As for the Jacobs family, they signed up to be implanted by a company called Applied Digital Solutions. The chip was called the VeriChip. Some—only half-jokingly—referred to it as "the Mark of the Beast." Incredibly, all three of the Stepford—sorry—*Jacobs* family were delighted to get chipped in a Boca Raton clinic. Chillingly, the process for the entire family took barely a couple of minutes. Applied Digital Solutions could not have been happier. The same went for Mr. and Mrs. Jacobs and their son. Fortunately, fifteen years down the line, the vast majority of the world's population has wisely avoided boldly going where the Jacobs went. Let's hope it stays that way.

The Media Gets Involved

While the staff of Applied Digital Solutions were congratulating themselves, not everyone was quite so enthused by this development. The BBC took a decidedly critical look at the situation: "The chips could also be used to contain personal information and even a global positioning device which could track a person's whereabouts, leading to fears the chip could be used for more sinister purposes." One can only assume that none of this ever crossed the minds of the Jacobs family. Maybe they just didn't care—which is even worse.

It wasn't just the BBC who raised a red flag. Very welcome commentary came from Dr. David M. Wood, the managing editor of *Surveillance and Society*, and Dr. Kirstie Ball, a lecturer in organization studies at Open University. In decidedly prophetic fashion, they predicted—in 2006—that by 2020 each and every one of us would find ourselves living in a world in which "our almost every movement, purchase and communication" will be monitored by "a complex network of interlinking surveillance technologies."

Well, as I write these words, 2020 is almost upon us. And guess what? Most of us *are* monitored 24/7. Not by chips (yet), but as a result of the fact that the vast majority of the world's population has a smartphone. It's not *literally* implanted in us, but take a look at the millions of people who can't keep their hands off their smartphone. It goes everywhere they go, even to the bathroom and to bed. Right now, it's just about the closest thing there is to an implant. And, just like a chip, a smartphone is one of the easiest things to hack into and monitor. If you have one, the NSA can monitor your every move—period. If your phone contains a boarding pass for a flight to Italy, the NSA will know where you are going and when. And that same agency has the ability to read those flirty text messages you're sending to a work colleague and behind your spouse's back.

The United Kingdom's information officer, Richard Thomas, echoed the warnings of Ball and Wood when he said that chips might, in the near future, be utilized "[by companies] who want to keep tabs on an employee's movements or by Governments who want a foolproof way of identifying their citizens—and storing information about them."

Enforcing the Implants

Now, we get to the most important and disturbing angle of all this: enforced implantation. It's one thing to be an idiot and agree to being implanted. But what if you, me—all of us—try to opt out? What will be the outcome for us? Jackbooted lackeys of the government kicking our doors down at 2:00 a.m. and whisking us away? *The American Dream's* Michael Snyder poses a relevant question: "What would you do if someday the government made it mandatory for everyone to receive an implantable microchip for identification purposes? Would you take it?"

All of us should strive to avoid such a disaster—and a disaster is undeniably what it would be. For everyone. We are many. They are not. All it would take is for everyone to shout out a collective "No!"

Snyder adds, "Once the government has microchips implanted in all of our soldiers, how long will it be before they want to put a microchip in all government employees for the sake of national security? Once the government has microchips in all government employees, how long will it be before they want to put a microchip in you?"

It's ironic that these questions are being discussed today in a serious fashion. Why so? Because in the 1990s, conspiracy theorist David Icke warned of this scenario coming true. He was dismissed by many—particularly the mainstream media—as a paranoid nut. History and recent developments have demonstrated that Icke was right on the money, though. As far back as 1994, Icke warned us something like this might happen:

The Brotherhood of the New World Order . . . want us bar-coded so we can be 'read' at supermarkets and banks, like a checkout assistant now reads a tin of beans. A man at IBM who invented the laser-bar reader for supermarkets has also developed a method of putting the same type of device under human skin in one billionth of a second. It is invisible to the naked eye and could carry all the information anyone needed to know about us. We could be permanently linked to a computer, and who is to say that signals could not be sent both ways?

One year later, he said this: "The game plan is known as the Great Work of Ages or the New World Order, and it seeks to introduce a world government to which all nations would be colonies; a world central bank and currency; a world army; and a microchipped population connected to a global computer. What is happening today is the culmination of the manipulation which has been unfolding for thousands of years."

So much for the past and present. But what of the future? To answer that question, we have to turn our attentions to the world of DARPA, the Defense Advanced Research Projects Agency.

"A Biological Authentication System"

DARPA's website bio reads as follows: "For more than fifty years, DARPA has held to a singular and enduring mission: to make pivotal investments in breakthrough technologies for national security." One of those "breakthrough technologies" is the implant. As in, the *human* implant. In 2013, DARPA revealed something amazing—but amazing in a disturbing, rather than positive, way. They were close to perfecting what they called an "edible authentication microchip." In essence, it would be a chip that would be swallowed rather than implanted. DARPA explained further that plans were being initiated to allow its scientists to place "a microchip inside a pill that users would swallow daily in order obtain the 'superpower' of having their entire body act as a biological authentication system for cellphones, cars, doors and other devices."

Whether or not we will see all of this come to fruition, or if there will be a backlash against the ever-growing culture of surveillance, very much remains to be seen. But what does all of this have to do with the world of alien abductions? The answer is: a great deal.

There can be no doubt that the idea extraterrestrials are implanting us with devices to control, manipulate, and perhaps even force us to perform sinister tasks is one of the most controversial aspects of the subject. But if, as we have just seen, the human race is now faced with being microchipped by our *own* kind—by leaders, in other words—it's actually not at all illogical or implausible that an alien race, an infinitely ancient group of extraterrestrials, might have done something almost identical in the distant past. Namely, perfected the very kinds of surveillance-based technologies that we are just now beginning to grasp.

21 MOTHMAN APOCALYPSE

One of the most disturbing aspects of the alien abduction phenomenon concerns the likes of Armageddon, the apocalypse, and end-of-the-world scenarios. It's a fact that numerous abductees have regular nightmares about the end of all things—nuclear destruction, an all-devastating Third World War, worldwide chaos. It was in 2017, however, that this particularly unsettling phenomenon reached its peak, with many people having graphic and horrific dreams of the atomic obliteration of the city of Chicago, Illinois.

And, in the process, it demonstrated that this link between alien abductions and worldwide disaster are of deep, secret interest to the US government—specifically the Department of Homeland Security. There is another aspect to this 2017 affair: the presence of a fiery-eyed, winged, humanoid monster seen soaring across the skies of Chicago. It was described by many eyewitnesses as closely resembling the legendary Mothman, a monstrous beast that plagued the people of Point Pleasant, West Virginia, from 1966 to 1967, and which culminated in massive tragedy, as you will now see.

The Dawning of the Mothman

In November 1966, sightings of a large, flying monster began in Point Pleasant, a small city located on the edge of the Ohio River. Witnesses described seeing something that resembled nothing less than a full-blown gargoyle: it was man-like in shape, about seven feet in height, and sported a pair of blazing eyes. Not surprisingly, it wasn't long before the people of Point Pleasant were caught up in a controversy filled with fear, supernatural activity, and terror. Animals went missing in town, others were found savagely mutilated. Townsfolk saw the grim-faced winged humanoid lurking in their yards, in the local woods, and in the crumbled remains of an old, Second World War–era explosives plant that for years dominated Point Pleasant's landscape.

For more than a year, the presence of the Mothman was not unlike that of a terrible albatross hanging over the heads of the residents. John Keel—a researcher and author on all things supernatural, and who wrote an acclaimed book on the saga, *The Mothman Prophecies*—spent a great deal of time in town and came across something chilling: feelings of dread among the people that something terrible was about to hit them. It did. On the night of December 15, 1967, Point Pleasant's Silver Bridge, which spanned the Ohio River, collapsed into the cold, deep waters, killing dozens of people. Almost instantly, the terrible disaster was associated with the presence of the Mothman—the theory being that it was either the cause of the destruction and death, or that it was an entity which had manifested in late 1966 to warn people of the then-looming cataclysm. Hardly surprising is the fact that, today, the Mothman is seen as a harbinger of doom. In almost seamless fashion, this all brings us to 2017, to the Mothman's presence in Chicago, and to the connections between alien abductions and the US government.

The Chicago Wave Heats Up

It was in early 2017 when the sightings of the Mothman in the skies above Chicago began. Over the course of the next few months, quite literally dozens of sightings were made of the strange creature. It was variously described as "a monster bat," "a large bird-like entity," and "a large winged being with bright red eyes." And then the dreams began: of the city of Chicago in ruins and millions dead. Hanging over the devastated city was a massive, ominous radioactive "mushroom cloud," the absolute calling card of a nuclear attack. Tensions and fears were rising, which is hardly surprising. It wasn't long before I received a number of reports of such chilling things.

On June 7, 2015, M.J. Banias wrote an article for Mysterious Universe titled "Chicago's Current Mothman Flap 'A Warning,' Says Expert." Banias described the wave of Mothman-type sightings in and around the city. The article quotes researcher Lon Strickler, who has looked into these particular cases: "There are many opinions as to why these sightings are occurring, including a general feeling that unfortunate events may be in the city's future. . . . At this point, I feel that this being may be attempting to distinguish a connection between locales within the city and future events. The witnesses have been very steadfast with what they have seen, and refuse to embellish on their initial descriptions. Each witness has had a feeling of dread and foreboding, which I believe translates into a warning of some type."

For me, it began in early August 2017.

The Abductees Speak of War and the End of the World

In the first week of August last year, a trio of people—all unconnected—messaged and emailed me with details of their experiences. One of those was an alien abductee named Kenny. A resident of San Bernardino, California, Kenny had a trauma-filled dream of a nuclear attack on the United States on the night of August 6. In the nightmare, Kenny was relaxing, watching television, in a house in a small town near Lubbock, Texas—a city he has not visited. Relaxation soon turned to absolute terror. A deep, thunderous rumbling suddenly filled the air. He raced to the front door, only to see a huge mushroom cloud hanging in the distance—perhaps five or six miles away, maybe more.

Kenny was frozen to the spot, unable to move, as the shock enveloped him that America had been hit by a devastating nuclear weapon. Then, as the blast from the detonation raced across the flat plains of West Texas, the sky turned dark and a massive wall of flame—perhaps two hundred feet high—destroyed everything in its wake. The last thing Kenny remembered before waking up in a frantic state was the sight of another explosion, this one right on Lubbock itself. The war to outdo all wars had begun. Civilization, Kenny knew, would soon be over.

Then, there was the story of Kimberly J. Her experience reached me just a couple of days after Kenny contacted me. Living in the heart of Chicago, Kimberly had heard of the growing sightings of the Mothman and, as an alien abductee herself, viewed the whole situation as scary and ominous. In her very own nightmare, Kimberly saw the destruction of Chicago by a nuclear weapon, with millions of people killed in seconds and the whole city destroyed. Most intriguing, Kimberly saw what she described as an approximately nine-foot-tall "bird-man" hovering over the radioactive remains and the terribly injured survivors of the initial blast. She got a feeling that the bird-man was "watching the end of us." It may well have been doing just that.

A Native American Connection Surfaces

As the days progressed, so did the reports. One of the people who contacted me was Chris O'Brien. He is an acclaimed researcher and writer on many unexplained phenomena, including the cattle mutilation controversy, which he covers in his 2014 book, *Stalking the Herd*. He said this to me:

Back in 2005 Grandfather Martin Gashweseoma, for many decades the "Fire Clan Prophecy Tablet" holder, spent a week with Naia and I at our home in Sedona, AZ. We had met him 10 years prior and we had become friendly with the then 83 year old Traditional Elder. During one conversation about the predicted "End of the Fourth World," I asked him how the dreaded "War of the Gourd of Ashes" would end. (In 1989, Martin announced the start of the final conflict would begin within the year and it did with "Desert Storm.") He said that North Korea would send fiery birds high in the sky to the US. I pressed him for further details suggesting maybe he meant China, and he said "No, Korea will be behind this attack, possibly w/ the help (or at the behest) of China." At the time Korea had no functioning nuclear weapons program and no ICBMs. As we all know, this has changed . . . Just thought I'd mention this!

Stephen Polak, who contacted me at the comments section at the Mysterious Universe website I regularly write for, provided a brief but thought-provoking comment: "As a Chicago resident myself who has recently had a dream of being consumed [by] an enormous wall of fire, I find all of this rather disquieting."

On August 12, I received yet another Facebook message of a similar nature, this one from Jacob, an American who is now a resident of Mulhouse, France. In Jacob's dream, an emergency broadcast message appeared on his TV screen, warning people to take cover: the nukes were flying. And that was it: just a few brief seconds of mayhem in the dream state. But it was still an undeniably nightmarish night for Jacob.

It must be said, it's not at all impossible that at least *some* of this may have been due to the growing tensions between North Korea and the United States. On August 9, 2017, the *Independent* ran an article on the North Korea issue that stated, in part, "While it's unclear if North Korea can successfully target US cities like Denver *and Chicago* with a nuclear ICBM, it's similarly unknown if US defence systems can strike it down—adding to American anxieties [italics mine]."

We Return to Whitley Strieber

Of particular interest is the fact that one of the most well-known figures in the realm of alien abductions also has a connection to the issues of Mothman and nuclear war—although, in his case, the connections were made decades ago. That man is Whitley Strieber, who, as we have seen, was the subject of intense surveillance from the late 1980s through the 1990s, and who wrote the best-selling alien abduction-themed book *Communion*.

It was at the height of all of the alien abductee/Chicago/nuclear war dreams that a friend in South Dakota, Jaime, contacted me. She had a very interesting piece of information that added more fuel to the fire. Jaime said that I really should read Strieber's 1984 novel, *Warday*, which was cowritten with James Kunetka. Although the story is fictional, the chief character in the book is Strieber himself.

It's a disturbingly engrossing story of a nuclear exchange between the former Soviet Union and the United States—an exchange which, thankfully, does not erupt into a full-scale, worldwide, nuclear war. But, even on a limited scale, the United States is left in a state of chaos with about 20 percent of the American population killed, and even more dying from the effects of blasts, burns, starvation, disease, and radiation poisoning. I asked Jaime what was so important about *Warday* in terms of the Mothman saga growing in Chicago. She wasted no time in telling me to reread pages 213–217. I did, and was stunned in the process. That portion of the book deals with a creature that sounds astonishingly like the Mothman: "There is a gigantic beast with bat wings and red, burning eyes that has attacked adults and carried off children. The creature stands seven feet tall and makes a soft whistling noise. It is often seen on roofs in populated areas, but only at night."

Strieber further writes, "I had just gotten off the Glendale trolley when I heard this soft sort of cooing noise coming from the roof of a house. The sound was repeated and I turned to look toward the house. Standing on the roof was what looked like a man wrapped in a cloak. Then it spread its wings and whoosh! it was right on top of me."

It's important to note—in light of the Mothman-like references—that *Warday* is not a piece of wild science fiction. The story of the winged monster is only included in the book to demonstrate how, in the aftermath of the war, strange and bizarre rumors surface and spread among the survivors. I did, however, find it intriguing that *Warday* makes a connection between a nuclear war and "a gigantic beast with bat wings and red, burning eyes." This is, of course, what is now being reported today. And let's not forget that Strieber is an alien abductee—one of the most famous and visible of all.

Rather notably, back in 1995 Strieber himself had a nightmare of a nuclear explosion which destroys Washington, DC in 2036—something which sees the end of the government as we know it today and the rise, in the wake of the disaster, of a dictatorship. In his 1997 book *The Secret School*, Strieber says of this dream (or of a brief view of what is to come via a future self) that: "Washington, D.C. is in ruins. However, this isn't the center of the memory. The center of the memory is that it was suddenly and completely destroyed by an atomic bomb, and nobody knows who detonated it."

"I, Too, Connected it with the Tensions in N Korea"

Then, on August 21, I received this from Jacqueline Bradley:

A few days ago I had a dream that several nuclear events occurred—in my dream. I remember the term "thermonuclear." There were several of these events popping up (appeared to be everywhere and small versions of what we would ordinarily be aware of). No one seemed to be very perturbed by these and people were just walking around, occasionally looking around and watching these.

Jacqueline continued:

I was aware that if you were caught up in one and died it killed off your soul or spirit too. All this was happening in broad daylight on sunny days. The dream ended where I was in some kind of alley with an old fashioned dustbin nearby. Suddenly I found myself "sinking" or evaporating and woke up. I wasn't scared by the dream, just puzzled. I too connected it with the tensions in N Korea. I've also been watching Twin Peaks and connected it with that, but not sure why.

"I Wonder If Any of These Dreams/Visions Were Preceded by an Abduction Event"

One day later, Jill S. Pingleton wrote to me:

As a paranormal investigator and student of metaphysics, I, like many, are concerned about the prophetic potential of so many having these dreams/visions. However as a former MUFON Chief Investigator, I'm wondering if the people reporting these dreams and associations are Contactees? . . . My point is that Contactees frequently recount stories of viewing scenes of mass destruction placed in their mind's eye during encounters with ETs. I don't know if they are being given glimpses of the future or only a possible time line unless events can be changed. Like a wake-up call to Contactees to get involved and speak out for the sake of humanity. Perhaps that's also the mission of the Mothman. I wonder if any of these dreams/visions were preceded by an abduction event or if it's part of an on going "download" that so many Contactees experience. I think much can be learned from studying the Experiencers/Witnesses. So many questions! Thank you for the articles and your insight into all these.

Having read Pingleton's words, I sincerely hoped that these dire images were indeed a wakeup call, rather than a literal glimpse into a terrible future.

The Accounts Continue with No Stopping in Sight

There was a notable Facebook message from a man named Andy, of the city of Manchester, England. Back in early June 2017, Andy had a dream of being in a deserted London. The city was not destroyed or in flames. It was, said Andy, "like they had all been evacuated," which is an interesting phrase to use. Well, I say the city was deserted. It was, except for two things: one was the sight of "a massive big black bird over [the Houses of] Parliament." Then, as Andy walked the streets, trying to figure out what had happened, he had that feeling we all get from time to time of being watched. He turned around to see a man in a black trench coat right behind him. The man was pale and gaunt, and—as Andy worded it—"had a funny smile." Andy's description sounds very much like a certain sinister MIB-like character in the saga of the Mothman—one Indrid Cold. Andy then woke up with his heart pounding, relieved that it had just been a dream. Or was it something more than just a dream?

Over at the Red Dirt Report website, Andrew W. Griffin wrote an article titled "Riders on the Storm (Strange Days Have Tracked Us Down)." In it, Griffin said, "Clearly we are entering very troubled waters. And it seems that the collective unconscious of humanity is clueing in that we are entering a perilous period in our history." Interestingly, he added that in relation to Kenny's dream of a nuclear bomb exploding near Lubbock, Texas, it was "not unlike my own dream that I wrote about on Jan. 26, 2017, which involved nuclear detonations near Joplin, Missouri."

Griffin expanded further:

We were in a car in the vicinity of Joplin, Missouri—something I noted in my mind in that it is on that nexus of high weirdness 37 degrees north and 94 degrees west (which I recently addressed here)—and nu-clear explosions, followed by menacing mushroom clouds, are going off at various intervals. . . . And yet as the nuclear blasts send radioactive debris through the town and infecting everything in its path, I seem to be the only one alarmed by what is happening around us. The whole experience has the feeling of a guided tour through a park or historic site. . . .

By late August, I had received a total of twenty-seven reports via Facebook, my blog, and email of the destruction of Chicago and other US cities. Of those twenty-seven, nineteen were from people in the United States, three were from Canada, two were from the United Kingdom, two were from Australia, and one was from Mexico. Of the twenty-seven nightmares, twenty-three of them had occurred in the previous three months.

Now, we come to the crux of the matter: the attention given to all of this by the Department of Homeland Security.

22 THE GOVERNMENT WANTS ANSWERS

Jayne is a woman who I have known since 2015. She has conscious recall of abductions dating back to childhood, which increased as she entered her mid- to late teens, and which reached a peak in her mid-thirties. At the time I write these words, Jayne is forty-one, and she lives in Chicago—which, as we just saw, was the scene of so many apocalyptic visions in 2017. Jayne has experienced the alien abduction phenomenon to an astonishing degree—she recalls that on five or six occasions she was abducted and taken onboard an alien craft, on which she was experimented and even shown a pair of hybrid children which she believes may have been hers.

It was on the night of April 11, 2008, when Jayne found herself yet again on a craft from another world. This time, though, she was not flat out on a table, as she'd often found herself in so many other incidents. She woke up to find herself in a large, comfortable chair. In no more than a couple of minutes, two young children were brought to her by a tall, skinny extraterrestrial entity with the ubiquitous large black eyes. Jayne felt that the being was trying to forge a connection between Jayne and the children, who were very pale-skinned and fragile looking, and whose eyes were completely black. Hybrids.

Although she found their appearance scary, Jayne admitted to feeling a bond—a significant bond. She was allowed to interact with the children—who, she estimated, were probably around seven or eight years old, and who had playful personalities. There was, however, a sense of unease on Jayne's part, which she felt was caused by their strange and unsettling appearances, rather than by any sense of hatred or malevolence on the part of the pair. The tall Grey stared intently as the three interacted for several hours, after which the children were taken away. Jayne did not see them again.

Now, let's jump to 2017.

The Weirdness Increases

Notably, in early 2017 Jayne experienced a series of strange phone calls. They ranged from hang-up calls in the middle of the night to weird electronic noises on the line, issues that were also central to the story John Keel told in relation to the Mothman sightings in Point Pleasant, West Virginia. On top of that, Jayne also found herself being followed several times by a skinny, tall Man in Black. Since Jayne works only two blocks from her apartment, she always walks to and from work. On the final occasion, at about seven in the evening, as she walked home after work, Jayne was confronted by the MIB. He stepped out of the shadows of the doorway and stood rigidly in front of her, displaying an unsettling grin. Jayne dodged passed him and raced to her apartment, which was just one block away. The strangest thing of all, however, was still to come.

Less than a week after the affair with the MIB, Jayne began to suffer from horrible nightmares. By now, you will likely have already deduced the nature of those nightmares. That's right: dreams of nuclear war, multiple American cities destroyed, millions of people dead, and an inferno-like Armageddon. Jayne was on edge for weeks after the dreams occurred, not knowing what to make of them, but keenly aware that numerous alien abductees had reported apocalyptic experiences.

In June 2017, on a Saturday morning, there was a knock on the front door of Jayne's apartment. Looking through the peephole, she saw a man in a suit—but definitely not one of the MIB—who she thought was probably in his mid-forties and whose hair was cut short. Her first thought was: Mormon. Her first thought was wrong. When Jayne opened the door she was confronted with a Department of Homeland Security ID. This was definitely not the way Jayne hoped to start her weekend. The man asked if he could come in. Jayne felt that she was hardly in a position to say no. So she invited him in. And so began one of the weirdest of all her UFO-related experiences.

A Government Agent Wants Answers

It's important to note that as an abductee, and as someone living in Chicago, Jayne knew all about the stories of the Mothman, and of the fears that the sightings were a warning of something cataclysmic to come. She also spent quite a bit of time discussing such matters on a Facebook group devoted to the alien abduction issue. Why is it so important? Simply because it appears that it was as a result of monitoring multiple such groups online that DHS came across Jayne and her experiences.

It's important to note that there was nothing particularly stressful or sinister about the meeting. The man was barely through the front door when he assured Jayne that she was not in any way in trouble. That was a relief. Jayne invited him to take a seat and made coffee for both of them. The agent of DHS came straight to the point: due to the nature of the work of the agency—helping to keep the United States protected from hostile forces and sources—a small group within the Department of Homeland Security had been tasked to investigate the growing reports of people having apocalyptic dreams of a nuclear nature, as well as the tie-in with the Mothman saga. As an aside, the man said that as this was a new and very alternative project for DHS, the handful of people on board had all read John Keel's *The Mothman Prophecies* and had "taken a look" at various online groups that were discussing the issues of bad dreams, North Korea, nuclear weapons, and the end of civilization.

The man further explained—"confided" might be a better word—to Jayne that her name had come up as a result of it being in the database of yet another agency, unnamed, which was "aware" of her UFO and alien abduction experiences. All attempts on Jayne's part to get the name of the agency turned out to be useless. Citing national security reasons, the man apologized, saying that he could not expand further on that issue. But he did want answers from Jayne.

Questions, Answers, and Nuclear Nightmares

The Department of Homeland Security, the man said, did not typically get involved in—and I quote Jayne's recollections—"*X-Files* things," except when national security was central to the matter. In this case, it most assuredly was. The man reeled off a number of questions about the history of Jayne's abduction experiences. She openly told him of her childhood encounters, her missing time experiences, and even the issue of the hybrid children and the Man in Black—all of which was preserved on a small digital recorder the man had brought with him, and which, said Jayne, she was fine with him using.

The man particularly wanted to know about the dreams: When did they begin? Was Jayne able to discern which cities were attacked in her dreams? How powerful were the weapons? Were the attacks small or large in scale? Did she have any idea which nation it was that had attacked the United States? Was there any indication in the dreams that America had been able to retaliate?

Jayne answered the questions as accurately as she could: The dreams had begun in the early part of March 2017. Chicago featured prominently in her nightmares, but not always. She also had a dream in which Seattle was annihilated. The weapons were clearly massively destructive, as Chicago was shown in her dreams to have been completely destroyed; there was hardly a soul left alive. She had fragments of memories that led her to believe the attack was initiated by China and North Korea, with some secret assistance from the Russians.

Rendering the United States Helpless

Most disturbing of all, Jayne believed that the attacking forces had somehow disabled the entire US military, thus leaving the nation completely open to attack. In her dreams, and two days before the attack, the internet went down, followed quickly by the collapse of every electrical device in the United States. The country was in a state of anarchy.

Jayne told the Department of Homeland Security agent that this was the one part of the dream she couldn't understand. Until, that is, she did some research online as to how such a thing might be achieved. She came across the matter of what is known as an electromagnetic pulse attack. For those who may not be aware of what this refers to, consider the words of Jean Baker McNeill and Richard Weitz, writing at The Heritage Foundation: "A major threat to America has been largely ignored by those who could prevent it. An electromagnetic pulse (EMP) attack could wreak havoc on the nation's electronic systems—shutting down power grids, sources, and supply mechanisms. An EMP attack on the United States could irreparably cripple the country."

And how might the nation be crippled? *Business Insider* correspondent Dave Mosher says that "nuclear EMPs—if a detonation is large enough and high enough—can cover an entire continent and cripple tiny circuits inside modern electronics on a massive scale, according to U.S. government reports. The power grid, phone and internet lines, and other infrastructure that uses metal may also be prone to the effects, which resemble those of a devastating geomagnetic storm."

According to Jayne, it was this issue—of the United States being destroyed as a result of enemy nations using EMP-driven technology, and then following up with a nationwide nuclear strike—which really caught the attention of her visitor from the government. Jayne felt that, given the somewhat slightly shocked look on his face, this was not the first time he had heard of this scenario.

The man went over several of the questions again, after which he thanked Jayne for her time. Notably, the man did not request that Jayne not talk about the interview. He simply thanked her and left. As for Jayne, she couldn't help but suspect that she was not the only person having nuclear nightmares who was getting a visit from the government. At the time of writing, Jayne's dreams are as regular as they are graphic. What might be going on in the offices of the Department of Homeland Security is a matter that is often at the forefront of her mind.

Jayne said to me, "Nick, I really hope they are on top of it." Me too. And so should you.

One last thing to ponder in relation to all this: in Whitley Strieber's 1984 novel, *Warday*, nuclear war begins with an electromagnetic pulse–based attack on the United States. Just perhaps, Strieber's story was not fiction, after all. Maybe, Strieber's mind unknowingly picked up on strands of future, catastrophic events—as so many other people may have done in Chicago and elsewhere in 2017.

CONCLUSIONS

Now, our strange search for the truth about what, precisely, government agencies know about the alien abduction phenomenon—and about the abductees, too—is at its end. Thanks to the provisions of the Freedom of Information acts of both the United States and the United Kingdom, we know with complete certainty that various military and intelligence agencies have opened secret files on countless people who have encountered otherworldly beings. The evidence, we know, dates back to the early 1950s. That was when the FBI quietly opened files on numerous people in the contactee field. They included George Adamski, George Van Tassel, Orfeo Angelucci, and Truman Bethurum. All of them—and many more too—came under the careful and secret scrutiny of J. Edgar Hoover's G-men.

Of course, the contactee experience didn't involve people being abducted against their will. For the most part, the so-called Space Brothers would invite amazed people onto their craft. Nevertheless, the phenomenon of the contactees is an important part of the overall story, chiefly because it demonstrates that the FBI was intrigued—and at times very concerned—by those who claimed face-to-face extraterrestrial–human interaction back in the fifties. But with a new decade looming large on the horizon, something changed the nature of how and why aliens interact with us. It was nothing positive. It was all negative. For us, at least.

The Space Brothers were benevolent, human-looking figures who wanted nothing more than to help steer us away from worldwide nuclear destruction and the extinction of life on Earth. This is in stark contrast to what erupted, all across the globe, just a few years after the likes of Van Tassel and Adamski were riding high. Suddenly, government agencies were faced with another nonhuman phenomenon—a very much unforeseen one. It was a phenomenon which concerned the governments of both the United States and the United Kingdom. At times, as we have seen, that concern was soon replaced by outright fear. A stark and chilling realization hit government agencies square in the face: strange creatures from faraway worlds were kidnapping citizens of this planet. People were being subjected to medical experiments of kinds which puzzled those tasked with studying the situation; memories were being wiped clean; and there was a new threat to national security. Forget the Russians: sinister entities from an entirely different realm of existence to ours were using us like cattle. And in the very early days—when the Betty and Barney Hill saga reached the media and the public—it seemed that nothing could be done to bring the onslaught to an end. Indeed, not only were government agencies confused and vulnerable to the activities of the new gang in town, but they were hit by a terrible realization that they were unable to do anything about the growing intrusion in our very midst.

In other words, in the early years of the alien enigma, agencies were still very much in the dark, doing their utmost to come to grips with something that overwhelmingly baffled them. The military was used to dealing with enemies that wanted to destroy us. The United States government knew that the Soviets were a major threat—and they knew how to handle them, in just the same way that the Soviets knew how to handle the Western world. The problem, though, as we have seen, is that the Grey abductors didn't act like regular enemies: they didn't attack us, they didn't destroy our cities in *Independence Day* style, and they never landed on the White

House lawn and demanded worldwide surrender. Rather, they acted in a stealthy, odd way which agencies—particularly the military—had a hard time coming to grips with. There was no outright aggression, but there was no friendly approach, either. So what did our leaders do? As we have seen, agencies took what they felt was the best approach possible—maybe even the only approach possible, taking into consideration the fact that the aliens were infinitely years ahead of us, in terms of science and technology.

There really was only one option available to governments. That was to watch—and watch closely—what was going on. To keep the abductees under *constant* surveillance. To stay fully aware of the growing alien abduction epidemic—at least to the extent they were able to. And to stand ready and prepared for any significant changes in the clandestine actions of the Greys.

This is why, as the 1960s became the 1970s, we saw the rise of the black helicopter and "phantom helicopter" phenomena. As we have seen, it was in the early 1970s that elements of the government secretly assigned a significant budget toward creating helicopter-based quick-reaction teams that could respond to alien abduction events, and monitor the homes of abductees across the United States. The project even used those same helicopters to try to figure out the connection between abductions and the cattle mutilation phenomenon. That encounters involving alien abductees and those mysterious helicopters are still being reported is a very good indication that this particular kind of aerial surveillance is still very much afoot.

And as the 1970s progressed and finally spilled over into the 1980s, we saw even more disturbing trends in the domain of alien abductions. People began reporting that they had been implanted by the aliens. They could feel the implants, just under their skin. But implanted with what, exactly? Small devices that potentially could monitor the movements of people—all across the United States and at any given moment. The fears were amplified when the government got wind that some abductees were also speculating that the Greys were planning to use the implanted victims of abduction in certain future events. The worrying inference was that possibly tens of thousands of abductees—maybe even more than that—would one day suddenly be "turned on" and used to sabotage the infrastructure of the United States: Manchurian candidates following the orders of their alien overlords—and in a slave-like style—as a result of those mysterious devices buried under their skin. Images and thoughts of something fairly close to a real-life version of the classic 1956 movie *Invasion of the Body Snatchers* were surely not too far behind.

There can be very little doubt at all that it was the rise of the implants angle which led the military and the intelligence world to take yet another step forward in the fight against the abduction phenomenon. That step was the dawning of the MILABS—the military's very own abductions. If the government couldn't get the answers to what was really going on by keeping a close watch on the UFO phenomenon itself, then they would take things a step or several further. In fact, not just a step or two but a series of gigantic leaps. The time finally came when the government decided to speak with the abductees directly.

As we have seen, such quiet and tactful approaches certainly occurred to a very small degree in the 1960s. But, decades later, things were very different. And things were getting weirder, too: alien abductees didn't have to just worry about being kidnapped by aliens. Now, they also had to deal with the military abducting them, too. And, in much the same way that the Greys would routinely wipe out people's memories, those running the MILAB programs would also used mind-altering technologies and drugs to get just about all of the information they needed from the abductees. By hook or by crook, they were going to get the answers. No wonder so many alien abductees feel like they are being used. *They are*, and in multiple ways—and by two groups with very different agendas: aliens and our very own government.

Let's not forget that there is an even stranger aspect to the MILAB controversy—an almost unbelievable one. It's the issue of MILAB teams fabricating abduction events—such as the trauma-filled Charles Hickson–Calvin Parker abduction late one night in October 1973 in Mississippi—

to try to place the aliens in an even more dangerous light than they already seem to be. Or, in the Brazilian affair of Antonio Villas Boas in October 1957, to make the whole abduction issue appear utterly ridiculous by bringing the issue of wild alien–human sex into the equation. As we have seen, many researchers of the UFO issue outright dismissed the Villas Boas story when it first surfaced, which was exactly what the government wanted: keep ufologists from investigating the *real* abductions by trying to convince them that all of the tales of alien abduction—and sex with extraterrestrials—were ludicrous and the works of hoaxers.

Things became even more worrying, from the government's perspective, when the issue of the human soul became a major factor in far more than a few alien abduction experiences. People spoke of their souls—their life force, their very essence—being violently ripped from their physical bodies. Others, like Whitley Strieber—who, as we have seen, was clearly the subject of deep government surveillance—spoke of the aliens telling him that they recycled human souls into new bodies and that the Greys had connections to the afterlife and the domain of the dead.

Bob Lazar—the controversial Area 51 whistleblower—spoke of reading highly classified files that talked about the aliens referring to us as "containers." Our bodies were not of primary interest to the Greys, the files stated. The Greys wanted our souls, the Area 51 documents revealed. This too was a major wake-up call for those in power who were struggling to keep the alien abduction issue in check, and to keep the public far away from the unsettling truth.

Bringing things right up to the present day, we are now seeing agents of various government, military, and intelligence bodies quietly approaching alien abductees and securing information—largely derived from dreams and nightmares—in relation to the likes of nuclear war and the actions of North Korea. And all tied in with the mysterious presence of the enigmatic Mothman, whose presence in 2017 in and around Chicago has led to fears that the city may be heading for Armageddon-like destruction, and all as a result of the crazed antics and threats of Kim Jong-un.

From the somewhat innocent—but admittedly still worrying—days of Betty and Barney Hill to the present era, we have seen the alien abduction issue alter and develop to an incredible degree, and at an alarming rate, too. And we see agencies of government doing all that they can—and, in the process, often struggling—to try to not just understand the full nature of the abductions but also find a way to stop the aliens' secret agenda.

So far, we have seen the various agencies of government and the military acting very much as what we might call a combined voyeur: carefully watching, listening, logging, probing, and collating data. How many secret files on alien abductees might be stored in vast warehouses, or in underground vaults, across not just the United States but the world itself, is anyone's guess.

All we can say for sure is that as long as the alien abduction phenomenon continues, highly classified files will continue to be compiled, studied, and stored in secure vaults. Black helicopters will continue to fly over the homes of American citizens, looking for leads and answers. Abductees will continue to be grilled and threatened by those running the military side of the situation: the MILABS. And a vast secret—that something unearthly is harvesting our souls and bodies for reasons not fully understood—will grow ever greater in size and scope, as governments struggle to hide the terrible, complicated truth from all of us.

It's a truth which officialdom won't come clean on—because they are deathly frightened to admit they don't know *how* to tell us.

ACKNOWLEDGMENTS

I would like to thank everyone at Red Wheel/Weiser, particularly Greg Brandenburgh, Eryn Carter, Mike Conlon, Kasandra Cook, Nicole Deneka, Jane Hagaman, Bonni Hamilton, and Kathryn Sky-Peck; my literary agent and good friend Lisa Hagan for her tireless work; and everyone who very generously shared their accounts of alien abduction with me.

BIBLIOGRAPHY

"1953 Hunrath and Wilkinson Disappearance." UFOBC, n.d. *http://www .ufobc.ca/kinross/planeMishaps/hunrathAndWilkinson.html.*

Adams, Tom. *The Choppers—and the Choppers: Mystery Helicopters and Animal Mutilations.* Paris, TX: Project Stigma, 1991.

Adamski, George. *Behind the Flying Saucer Mystery.* New York: Paperback Library Edition, 1967.

"Animal Mutilation." *FBI Records: The Vault,* n.d. *https://vault.fbi.gov/ Anmal%20Mutilation. 2017.*

Associated Press. "Family Implanted with Computer Chips." *USA Today,* May 10, 2002. *http://usatoday30.usatoday.com/tech/ news/2002/05/10/implantable-chip.htm.*

Baker McNeill, Jenna, and Richard Weitz. "Electromagnetic Pulse (EMP) Attack: A Preventable Homeland Security Catastrophe." The Heritage Foundation, October 20, 2008. *http://www.heritage.org/home land-security/report/electromagnetic-pulse-emp-attack-preventable homeland-security-catastrophe.*

Banias, MJ. "Chicago's Current Mothman Flap 'A Warning,' Says Expert." Mysterious Universe, June 7, 2017. *http://mysteriousuniverse .org/2017/06/chicagos-current-mothman-flap-a-warning-says-expert/.*

"Barcode Everyone at Birth." BBC, November 18, 2014. *http://www.bbc .com/future/story/20120522-barcode-everyone-at-birth.*

Beckley, Timothy. *The UFO Silencers: Mystery of the Men in Black.* New Brunswick, NJ: Inner Light Publications, 1990.

Beckley, Timothy, and Christa Tilton. *Underground Bio Lab at Dulce: The Bennewitz UFO Papers.* New Brunswick, NJ: Inner Light Productions, 2012.

Bennett, Colin. *Looking for Orthon: The Story of George Adamski, the First Flying Saucer Contactee, and How He Changed the World.* New York: Paraview Press, 2001.

Bishop, Greg. *Project Beta: The Story of Paul Bennewitz, National Security, and the Creation of a Modern UFO Myth.* New York: Paraview-Pocket Books, 2005.

Bishop, Greg, and Wesley Nations. "Interview: Karla Turner: Don't Exclude the Anomalous." In *Wake Up Down There! The Excluded Middle Collection*, edited by Greg Bishop, 91–100. Kempton, IL: Adventures Unlimited Press, 2000.

Bishop, Jason III. "The Dulce Base." Sacred Texts, n.d. *http://www.sacred-texts.com/ufo/dulce.htm.*

Blum, Ralph, and Judy Blum. *Beyond Earth: Man's Contact with UFOs.* New York: Bantam Books, 1977.

Booher, David. *No Return: UFO Abduction or Covert Operation?* San Antonio, TX: Anomalist Books, 2017.

Booth, Billy. "1987—The Ilkley Moor Alien Photograph." Thought Co., March 18, 2017. *https://www.thoughtco.com/the-ilkley-moor-alien-photograph-3293364.*

Branton. "The Dulce Book." Whale, n.d. *http://www.whale.to/b/dulce_b.html.*

Bryan, Charles W. "What Was Operation Plowshare?" How Stuff Works, April 28, 2016. *http://www.stuffyoushouldknow.com/podcasts/what-was-operation-plowshare.htm.*

"Christa Tilton." *Willow Andreasson's Journey into the Mysteries of Life*, November 19, 2016. *https://willowandreasson.wordpress.com/tag/christa-tilton/.*

"The Christa Tilton Story." Ufocasebook, n.d. *http://www.ufocasebook.com/ christatilton.html. 2017.*

Chua, Philip. "Bar Code for Humans?" Inquirer.net, December 9, 2013. *http://newsinfo.inquirer.net/543137/bar-code-for-humans.*

Coleman, Loren. *Mothman and Other Curious Encounters.* New York: Paraview Press, 2002.

Conroy, Ed. *Report on Communion: The Facts Behind the Most Controversial True Story of Our Time.* New York: Avon Books, 1989.

Corso, Philip J., and William J. Birnes. *The Day after Roswell.* New York: Simon & Schuster, 1997.

Creighton, Gordon. "The Amazing Case of Antonio Villas Boas." In *The Humanoids*, edited by Charles Bowen, 187–199. Chicago: Henry Regnery Company, 1969.

Crystall, Ellen. *Silent Invasion.* New York: St. Martin's, 1991.

Cutchin, Joshua. *A Trojan Feast.* San Antonio, TX: Anomalist Books, 2015.

Defense Advanced Projects Research Agency. *http://www.darpa.mil/.*

Faletto, Joanie, ed. "Allegedly There Is a Secret Underground Alien Base in Dulce, New Mexico." *Curiosity Makes You Smarter*, August 11, 2017. *https://curiosity.com/topics/the-alleged-secret-underground-alien-base-in dulce-new-mexico-curiosity/.*

Fawcett, Lawrence, and Barry J. Greenwood. *Clear Intent: The Government Cover-Up of the UFO Experience.* Englewood Cliffs, NJ: Prentice-Hall, 1984.

Federal Bureau of Investigation files on George Adamski, declassified under the terms of the United States Freedom of Information Act.

Federal Bureau of Investigation files on George Hunt Williamson, declassified under the terms of the United States Freedom of Information Act.

Federal Bureau of Investigation files on George Van Tassel, declassified under the terms of the United States Freedom of Information Act.

Federal Bureau of Investigation files on Karl Hunrath, declassified under the terms of the United States Freedom of Information Act.

Fowler, Raymond E. *The Andreasson Affair: The Documented Investigation of a Woman's Abduction Aboard a UFO.* Englewood Cliffs, NJ: Prentice-Hall, 1979.

———. *The Andreasson Affair—Phase Two: The Continuing Investigation of a Woman's Abduction by Extraterrestrials.* Mill Spring, NC: Wild Flower Press, 1994.

———. *The Andreasson Legacy—UFOs and the Paranormal: The Startling Conclusion of the Andreasson Affair.* New York: Marlowe & Company, 1997.

———. *The Watchers: The Secret Design Behind UFO Abduction.* New York: Bantam Books, 1990.

———. *The Watchers II: Exploring UFOs and the Near-Death Experience.* Newberg, OR: Wild Flower Press, 1995.

Friedman, Stanton T., and Kathleen Marden. *Captured! The Betty and Barney Hill UFO Experience.* Wayne, NJ: New Page Books, 2007.

Fuller, John G. *The Interrupted Journey: Two Hours "Aboard a Flying Saucer."* New York: The Dial Press, 1966.

Gerhard, Ken. *Encounters with Flying Humanoids.* Woodbury, MN: Llewellyn Publications, 2013.

Good, Timothy. *Alien Liaison: The Ultimate Secret.* London: Arrow Books, 1992.

Griffin, Andrew W. "Riders on the Storm (Strange Days Have Tracked Us Down)." *Red Dirt Report*, November 10, 2016. *http://www.redirtreport.com/red-dirt-grit/riders-storm-strange-days-have-tracked-us-down.*

Hapgood, Sarah. "The Aveley Abduction." *sjhstrangetales*, January 30, 2012. *https://sjhstrangetales.wordpress.com/2012/01/30/the-aveley-abduction/.*

Hickson, Charles, and William Mendez. *UFO Contact at Pascagoula.* Tucson, AZ: Wendelle C. Stevens Publishing, 1983.

Hopkins, Budd. *Intruders: The Incredible Visitations at Copley Woods.* New York: Ballantine Books, 1987.

————. *Missing Time.* New York: Ballantine Books, 1981.

"Horn Island Chemical Warfare Service Quarantine Station." Wikipedia, August 31, 2017. *https://en.wikipedia.org/wiki/Horn_Island_Chemical_Warfare_Service_Quarantine_Station.*

Howe, Linda Moulton. *An Alien Harvest: Further Evidence Linking Animal Mutilations and Human Abductions to Alien Life Forms.* Littleton, CO: Linda Howe Productions, 1989.

"The Ilkley Moor (Philip Spencer) Alien Abduction." Mysteries: Fact, Fiction and Conjecture, n.d. *http://www.factfictionandconjecture.ca/files/ilkley_moor.html.*

Jacobs, David. *The Threat.* New York: Simon & Schuster, 1999.

————. *Walking Among Us: The Alien Plan to Control Humanity.* San Francisco: Disinformation Books, 2015.

Jordan, Debbie, and Kathy Mitchell. *Abducted!* New York: Dell Publishing, 1994.

Keel, John A. *The Mothman Prophecies.* New York: Tor, 2002.

Keith, Jim. *Black Helicopters over America: Strikeforce for the New World Order.* Lilburn, GA: IllumiNet Press, 1994.

————. *Black Helicopters II: The Endgame Strategy.* Lilburn, GA: IllumiNet Press, 1997.

Kerner, Nigel. *Grey Aliens and the Harvesting of Souls: The Conspiracy to Genetically Tamper with Humanity.* Rochester, VT: Bear & Company, 2010.

————. *The Song of the Greys.* London: Hodder & Stoughton, 1997.

Leslie, Desmond, and George Adamski. *Flying Saucers Have Landed.* London: Werner Laurie, 1953.

Lorenzen, Coral E., ed. "Soldier Sees Flash: Unconscious 24 Hours." The *A.P.R.O. Bulletin* (March 1959). *http://www.openminds.tv/pdf/apro/apro_mar_1959.pdf.*

Lorenzen, L. J. "Where Is Private Irwin?" *Flying Saucers.* November 1962.

Mack, John E. *Abduction: Human Encounters with Aliens.* New York: Ballantine Books, 1994.

————. *Passport to the Cosmos: Human Transformation and Alien Encounters*. New York: Three Rivers Press, 1999.

Marden, Kathleen, and Denise Stoner. *The Alien Abduction Files: The Most Startling Cases of Human-Alien Contact Ever Reported*. Wayne, NJ: New Page Books, 2013.

Meghan, Neal. "Is a Human 'Barcode' on the Way?" *New York Daily News*, June 1, 2012. *http://www.nydailynews.com/news/national/human-barcode-society-organized-invades-privacy-civil-liberties-article-1.1088129*.

"Microchip Mind Control, Implants and Cybernetics." Rense.com, December 6, 2001. *http://www.rense.com/general17/imp.htm*.

"A Microchipped Population—David Said This Was Coming 12 Years Ago and Here It is Folks!" Red Ice Creations, October 23, 2004. *http://www.redicecreations.com/news/2004/microicke.html*.

Mosher, Dave. "Nuclear Bombs Trigger a Strange Effect that Can Fry Your Electronics—Here's How it Works." Business Insider, June 7, 2017. *http://www.businessinsider.com/nukes-electromagnetic-pulse-electronics-2017-5*.

Newling, Dan. "Britons 'Could Be Microchipped Like Dogs in a Decade.'" *Daily Mail*, October 30, 2006. *http://www.dailymail.co.uk/news/article-413345/Britons-microchipped-like-dogs-ecade.html*.

O'Brien, Christopher. *Stalking the Herd: Unraveling the Cattle Mutilation Mystery*. Kempton, IL: Adventures Unlimited Press, 2014.

"Project Gasbuggy Atomic Explosion Site." Roadside America.com, n.d. *https://www.roadsideamerica.com/story/16912*.

Randles, Jenny. *Alien Contacts & Abductions: The Real Story from the Other Side*. New York: Sterling Publishing, 1993.

Reynolds, Rich. "The Villas Boas Event." *The UFO Reality*, January 11, 2006. *http://ufor.blogspot.com/2006/01/villa-boas-event.html*.

Rogo, Scott, ed. *Alien Abductions: True Cases of UFO Kidnappings*. New York: NAL Books, 1990.

Sauder, Richard. *Underground Bases and Tunnels: What Is the Government Trying to Hide?* Kempton, IL: Adventures Unlimited Press, 1997.

———. *Underwater and Underground Bases.* Kempton, IL: Adventures Unlimited Press, 2001.

"Shamanistic Order to Be Established Here." *L.A. Times*, April 8, 1934.

Snyder, Michael. "After the Government Microchips Our Soldiers, How Long Will it Be Before They Want to Put a Microchip in YOU." Activist Post, May 8, 2012. *https://www.activistpost.com/2012/05/after-government-microchips-our.html.*

Strieber, Whitley. *Breakthrough: They Are Here . . . with a Message of Hope.* New York: Harper Spotlight, 1995.

———. *Communion: A True Story.* New York: Beach Tree Books, 1987.

———. *Confirmation: The Hard Evidence of Aliens Among Us.* New York: St. Martin's Press, 1998.

———. *The Secret School.* NewYork: Pocket Books, 1997.

———. *Transformation: The Breakthrough.* New York: Avon Books, 1988.

———. *Warday.* New York: Warner Books, 1985.

Strieber, Whitley, and Anne Strieber. *The Communion Letters.* London: Pocket Books, 1997.

Stringfield, Leonard H. *Situation Red: The UFO Siege.* London: Sphere Books, 1978.

Szymanksi, Greg. "Plans to Microchip Every Newborn in US and Europe Underway—Former Chief Medical Officer of Finland." Rense. com, May 11, 2006. *http://www.rense.com/general71/under.htm.*

Tilton, Christa. *The Bennewitz Papers.* New Brunswick, NJ: Inner Light Publications, 1994.

Turner, Karla. *Into the Fringe: A True Story of Alien Abduction.* New York: Berkeley Books, 1992.

United Kingdom Government files on Anne Leamon, 1962: AIR 2/16918.

United Kingdom Government files on Diane Foulkes, 1962: AIR 2/17984.

United Kingdom Government files on Ronald Wildman, 1962: AIR 2/16918.

United Kingdom Government Home Office files on mysterious helicopters: HO 371/74/94, "Alleged Unauthorized Helicopter Flights in Derbyshire and Cheshire." March, 1974.

United Kingdom Government Special Branch files on the Aetherius Society. 1958–1959.

United States Air Force files on Betty and Barney Hill, declassified under the terms of the United States Freedom of Information Act.

"US Family Gets Health Implants." BBC News, May 11, 2002. *http://news .bbc.co.uk/2/hi/health/1981026.stm.*

Valerian, Valdamar. *Matrix II.* Las Vegas: Leading Edge, 1991.

Walton, Travis. *Fire in the Sky.* Boston: Da Capo Press, 1997.

Watson, Paul Joseph. "Ex-DARPA Head Wants You to Swallow ID Microchips." Infowars, January 7, 2014. *http://www.infowars.com/ ex-darpa-head-wants-you-to-swallow-id-microchips/.*

Williamson, George Hunt. Letter to Frank Gibson, March 5, 1954.

———. *Other Voices.* Wilmington, DE: Abelard Productions, 1995.

———. *Road in the Sky.* Aylesbury, UK: Futura Books, 1975.

———. *Traveling the Path Back to the Road in the Sky.* New Brunswick, NJ: Inner Light Publications, 2012.